A YANK AT CAMBRIDGE

B.H. HOWELL:
THE FORGOTTEN CHAMPION

A YANK AT CAMBRIDGE

B.H. HOWELL:
THE FORGOTTEN CHAMPION

BY
GÖRAN R BUCKHORN

A HTBS PUBLICATION

Published by 'Hear The Boat Sing' (HTBS)
42 Pearl Street
Mystic, Connecticut 06355-1830
USA
www.heartheboatsing.com
@boatsing

ISBN 978-0-578-16289-8

To contact HTBS or the author, please use e-mail:
heartheboatsing@gmail.com

Book design by Göran R Buckhorn, with the help of Dayna Carignan

Cover design: Dayna Carignan

Front cover: Hunting Howell, Trinity Hall BC. (From the Benjamin Hunting Howell photo album. Courtesy of the National Rowing Foundation.)

Back cover: The Trinity Hall crew, winners of the 1897 Head of the River. (Courtesy of the Master and Fellows of Trinity Hall, Cambridge University.)

In memory of
William Hartwell "Hart" Perry, Jnr,
23 August 1933 – 3 February 2011

When the waves rise high and higher as they toss about together,
And the March-winds, loosed and angry, cut your chilly heart in two,
Here are eighteen gallant gentlemen who come to face the weather
All for valour and for honour and a little bit of blue!

From the poem "A Little Bit of Blue" by R. C. Lehmann

TABLE OF CONTENTS

Bill East in a double scull with his younger brother, ready to coach
Hunting Howell in his single scull.

Preface

In the spring of 2009, the National Rowing Foundation (NRF), with its headquarters in Connecticut, received a remarkable gift: an old album of rowing photographs which had once belonged to the American oarsman Benjamin Hunting Howell. The donor was Frederick Elliott, who had received the album from some relatives. Elliott's step-grandmother was Hunting Howell's niece, Juliette Katherine Howell Brandi, the daughter of the oarsman's brother, James Rapelje Howell. The reason Elliott was given these photographs was the rowing connection he had with Howell – and it was not just any simple aquatic link, it was the world's most famous rowing regatta, Henley Royal Regatta in Henley-on-Thames, England.

Howell represented Trinity Hall Boat Club ('the Hall'), Cambridge University, and later the Tideway club Thames Rowing Club at Henley between 1895 and 1900, while Elliott rowed for Kent School, Connecticut, in the 1972 Princess Elizabeth's Challenge Cup at Henley. Elliott and his fellow members of the crew wrote history that year by taking the cup. One of the oarsmen in the Kent boat, Rick Rinehart, wrote a book about their Henley adventure, *Men of Kent: Ten Boys, a Fast Boat, and the Coach Who Made Them Champions*, which was published in 2010.

The 'coach' whom Rinehart refers to in the book title was William Hartwell 'Hart' Perry, Jnr. He was an extraordinary man who had rowed; coached; been the president of the National Association of Amateur Oarsmen (N.A.A.O., the predecessor organisation to today's USRowing); and had been an official at national and international rowing events: in two Olympic Games, ten World Rowing Championships and 18 World Rowing Junior Championships. Perry, who was the first non-Commonwealth citizen elected a Henley Steward in December 1974, had been the executive director of the NRF for a long time. It was in this position that he had received the Hunting Howell photo album from the hands of his former oarsman, Frederick Elliott. It is a grave understatement to say that Perry was 'grateful' to accept the album on behalf of the NRF; instead he was euphoric, or, at least, he was when he showed it to me a couple of weeks after he had received it from Elliott.

The photographs in the Hunting Howell photo album are beautiful, unique and really a wonderful statement about England in the late 1890s. They were taken between 1896 and 1899, and most of the 31 pictures, all in black & white, are large, measuring 11 x 8 ½ in. (27.94 x 21.59 cm). A few of them have a mark saying 'Messrs. Stearn, Cambridge', who must be Thomas Stearn. He established a photography studio at 72 Bridge Street, Cambridge, ca. 1866, and was later joined in his business by his sons, Henry, Walter, James and Rupert. Howell is in all of the photographs but five, and some of them show him sculling in the Diamond Challenge Sculls at Henley and in the Wingfield Sculls – The Amateur Sculling Championships of the Thames and Great Britain on the River Thames in London. There are also some wonderful photographs from social events and group photos with Howell and his fellow undergraduates at Trinity Hall. It is easy to understand why Hart Perry loved this album. I, too, became thrilled with these photographs.

Perry told me that Hunting Howell, who was born and raised in a well-to-do family in New York, is unknown to the American sport world of today, even among many rowing historians. This is probably because he only rowed and sculled for a few years – and in England. It is noteworthy that despite Howell's short rowing career, he won the Grand Challenge Cup in 1895, slightly more than half a year after he pulled an oar for the first time. He also won the Diamonds and the Wingfields in 1898 and 1899. Without doubt Howell was a very talented oarsman and furthermore, he had what was known as 'pluck', courage and fighting spirit.

As the head of the NRF, which is the organisation that inducts members into the NRF's National Rowing Hall of Fame, Perry thought that Howell, with his prominent victories, had proved to be a worthy member of the Rowing Hall of Fame. But Perry needed more information about this exceptional oarsman and his races across the pond before he could suggest Hunting Howell's name to the NRF's selection board of the Rowing Hall of Fame. Perry asked me to dig out what I could find about Howell in archives and on the Internet. It was with great excitement I began the project in the summer of 2009.

Although it was a slow process, I managed to feed Perry some good stories now and then, and I constantly kept him in the loop with the ups and downs of my research. When my rowing history blog 'Hear The Boat Sing' (HTBS) really took off in 2010, I got side-tracked, but never derailed from the 'Hunting Howell project'. However, when the news reached me in the early afternoon of 3 February 2011 that Hart Perry had died an hour earlier, the project came to an immediate standstill. Nevertheless, I gradually started up the project again in the autumn of 2012. It was also then I decided to publish my research.

I feel that it is crucial to explain a couple of things with this little book: it has proven necessary to keep my writing within certain limits. This is a brief 'rowing biography' about Hunting Howell and some of his contemporary oarsmen, among them 'Old Blues' from Oxford and Cambridge, amateur and professional scullers, legendary rowing coaches and rowing scribes. It has been difficult to track down information about Howell after his short rowing career came to an end in 1900.

Benjamin Hunting Howell was known as Hunting, despite the fact that the rest of the male line for generations had spelled the middle name, or as a last name, with two 't's – Huntting. In numbers of newspaper articles about him and books where he is mentioned, he goes by the name of 'B. H. Howell' and, in another few, as 'Hunting Howell'. In the photo album mentioned previously, where small notes are scribbled beneath the photographs, he is named 'Hunting' so I decided to go with this spelling.

Finally, it is with great sadness I write that I wished that Hart Perry had lived to see this book completed. I hope it shows that Perry was right about Hunting Howell – he was an astonishing oarsman. If Howell thereby is a candidate for the NRF's Rowing Hall of Fame, one hundred and fifteen years after his rowing career ended, it is not for me to say. My work is done; for me it only remains to dedicate this book in memory of my friend and mentor, Hart Perry.

G.R.B.
Mystic, April 2015

CHAPTER 1
The Forgotten Champion

In the 2 July 1938 issue of *The New Yorker*, there was a short article about rowing. This was indeed a rare thing, though the magazine had published articles on rowing before and, during the late 1920s and the 1930s, had some drawings depicting the Yale-Harvard Race on its cover. The unsigned piece in the July 1938 issue, with the title "Forgotten Champion", was a small scoop as it told the readers that:

> When speaking of the famous regatta at Henley-on-Thames, England, which has its hundredth birthday this week, it's customary for sportswriters to mention that only two Americans have ever won the Diamond Sculls, a singles event over the mile-and five-six-tenths (Henley) course. They are, the papers would have you know, Edward Ten Eyck (1897), member of a family distinguished in crew history, and Walter Hoover (1922), whose family has no particular historical connections.

Despite using the word 'crew' as a synonym for 'rowing', an American custom little understood by non-Americans, the article was from a rowing history point of view very interesting. The American sculler who won the trophy of the Diamond Challenge Sculls in between Edward Hanlan Ten Eyck and Walter Hoover, the article stated, was 'B. Hunting Howell, who not only deserves to be listed with Ten Eyck and Hoover but moreover outranks them both by virtue of having won the coveted trophy twice. It was in 1898 and 1899, to be exact'.

Benjamin Hunting Howell – A Yank at Cambridge oars.

Who then was this sculler, B. Hunting Howell, the 'forgotten champion', whom *The New Yorker* so highly praised?

Benjamin Hunting Howell was born on 3 September 1875 in Brooklyn, New York. His father was Frederick Huntting Howell (1848-1929) and his mother Katherine 'Katie' Van Liew Howell (1853-1911), who came from an old Dutch family. The Huntting Howells were originally Long Islanders and some of them had founded the town of Southampton, Suffolk County, Long Island, in the 1640s. The maternal line of the family was originally from Holland who, via England, had immigrated early to the United States, while the paternal line came from Wales – in brief, the Huntting Howells were real Yankees.

Hunting Howell's grandfather, Benjamin Huntting Howell (1811-1900), had moved from Long Island to Brooklyn to become a prominent merchant. He was named after his maternal grandfather, the Revolutionary War Colonel Benjamin Huntting, who had served under General George Washington and fought bravely at the Battle of Long Island in August 1776.

Between 1843 and 1858 Benjamin Huntting Howell ran his grocery firm B. H. Howell & Company. For a short stint he was also president of an insurance company until he co-founded B. H. Howell

& Son together with his son Thomas A. Howell in 1861. The firm soon flourished and made good profit from buying and selling molasses and sugar, eventually becoming one of the largest companies in the trade in the United States. In 1870, two more sons, Frederick Huntting Howell and Henry Banks Howell (the latter a son from a second marriage), joined the company, whereupon it again changed its name, now to B. H. Howell, Son & Company, Inc. The company later took up another relative, James Howell Post, as a partner.

At the death of Benjamin Huntting Howell in 1900, a re-organization of the company was made into the National Sugar Refining Company of New Jersey. Post became president of the concern, which in the next decades would be one of the largest companies in the sugar trade in the world.

It is clear that Hunting and his younger siblings, his sister Erla Louise (1876-1975) and brother James Rapelje (1879-1960), had a comfortable upbringing where all their needs were taken care of by servants.

Their father, Frederick Howell, collected art and patronized 'coming' American painters. It was probably his brother, Thomas Howell, who introduced him to the artist William Merritt Chase. After studies at the Academy of Fine Arts in Munich, Germany, and travels around Europe, Chase had set up a studio at the so-called Tenth Street Studio Building at 51 West 10th Street in Greenwich Village, New York City. Soon his portrait paintings became popular and many businessmen in New York had him painting their wives and children, among them also Frederick Howell, who became an early collector of Chase's artwork. According to the William Merritt Chase expert Ronald G. Pisano, in the beautiful book *William Merritt Chase – Portraits in Oil* (2007), in 1886, Howell commissioned Chase to paint his wife and to make one painting each of their three children. The paintings of Katie, Erla and Rapelje are now in private collections, while the whereabouts of the painting of Hunting is not known.

From an old photograph we know that the painting of young Hunting shows him with long, dark hair; he is dressed in a velvet jacket with an enormous belt and he wears a big hat with a white plume.

Long spats cover his legs and he wears large leather gloves. His right hand rests on the neck of a greyhound. However, from another old photograph of the salon in the Howells' residence at 49 West 46th Street, showing the three paintings of the Howell children, the one of Hunting looks slightly different from the photograph of him and the dog. The painting in the salon shows Hunting holding a long staff with a white ribbon in his right hand – and no trace of the dog.

Little is otherwise known about Hunting's childhood. It is said that Katie Van Liew Howell took her children to Europe when they were quite young, both to Paris and London. In the British capital, she bought a house and spent large parts of her life there.

Around 1890, Hunting was signed up at the Pennsylvania Military Academy (later called Pennsylvania Military College) in the town of Chester, Pennsylvania.

In the autumn of 1894, Hunting was admitted to the college Trinity Hall, Cambridge, in England. Nowhere is it indicated that the Huntting Howells had any previous ties to Trinity Hall or Cambridge University. Hunting's younger brother would follow him there three years later. By then, their father ran his business from an office in London and was living at 27 Portman Square in London, while when Hunting was admitted to Trinity Hall, Frederick Howell's address was given as 109 Wall Street, New York.

Trinity Hall, the fifth-oldest college of Cambridge University, was founded in 1350 by William Batesman, the Bishop of Norwich. It was from the Bishop's coat of arms that Trinity Hall got its coat of arms, a crescent, which the oarsmen in the college boat club, Trinity Hall BC, or just 'the Hall', would wear on their white boat club jackets which had a black trim, or on their white jerseys with a black trim when they were boating on the River Cam.

In the beginning, the colleges in Cambridge were known as Halls or Houses, and some of them would later officially change their names to 'College'. When the nearby Trinity College was established in 1546, Trinity Hall had to keep its name. Trinity Hall was, and still is, a fairly small institution beautifully situated by the Cam. The author Henry James once said: 'If I were called upon to mention the prettiest corner of the world, I should draw a thoughtful sigh and point the way to the gardens of Trinity Hall'.

4

An advertisement in *The Century Illustrated Monthly Magazine* in August 1886 for the Pennsylvania Military Academy in Chester, Pennsylvania, where Hunting studied before going to Trinity Hall. According to this advertisement, the military system was 'second only to that of West Point'. The college was founded in 1821 as the Bullock School for Boys and would change names and locations several times. One of its most famous alumni was the film director, Cecil B. DeMille.

Although Trinity Hall was a charming spot by the Cam, the river itself was murky. After a cleaning job in the mid-1890s, the journalist and writer Bertie Fletcher Robinson, who had rowed at Jesus College, wrote that, 'despite the fact that a new drainage system has partially cleaned its muddy waters, it is still far from a thing of beauty'.

Hunting Howell had never rowed competitively in America, and little did he know when he arrived to Trinity Hall what an impact the Cam would have on his life during his years at Cambridge.

According to James Douglas, in his *Rowing on the Cam* (1977), the 'new sport' of rowing, or boat racing as it was called during its early years, came to the Cam in 1825. The first boat club on the Cam was Johnian Boat Club (St. John's College), which was later called Lady Margaret Boat Club. It was followed by First Trinity (Trinity College), and soon thereafter a few other colleges followed, among

5

The Arms of Trinity Hall, Wills's Cigarettes, a tobacco card from 1922.

them Trinity Hall in 1827. By 1828, when Cambridge University Boat Club (CUBC) was founded, Jesus, Caius, Corpus Christie, Magdalene and Emmanuel also had boats on the river.

However, some of the colleges' boats appeared, disappeared and then re-appeared again on the river and in races during these early years, according to *The Bumps: An Account of the Cambridge University Bumping Races 1827 – 1999* (2000) by John Durack, George Gilbert and John Marks. As the River Cam has always been, the authors write, 'a most unlikely river on which to organise rowing races; narrow, winding and weedy', the Cambridge colleges' races have been to chase and hit ('bump') each other, as the Cam has never allowed two or more boats racing abreast. The boat that stays ahead during several days of racing without being bumped takes the headship and becomes the Head of the River.

In the book *The Jesus College Cambridge Boat Club 1827-1962* (1962) by Frederick Brittain and Humphrey B. Playford, the authors quote an 1828 article from the *Sporting Magazine* about a bump race on the Cam that year: 'The boating at Cambridge was miserable work. The boats were well manned, of course, as they had the flower of Westminster and Eton to pick from; but the farce of a boat-race

The Main Entrance of Trinity Hall in Trinity Lane, a postcard from the 1910s.

The Front Court of Trinity Hall, a postcard from the 1910s.

A bump at the Lent Races.

upon a river which will not in most places admit of two boats abreast is too absurd'.

This racing model, bump racing, was developed at Oxford – as early as in 1815 – where the River Isis is almost as narrow as the Cam. Just as there are two different periods for bump races at Oxford, Torpids in the beginning of March and Eights Week, or Summer Eights, in May, Cambridge has Lent Races, or Lent Bumps, at the end of February or beginning of March and May Bumps, or May Races, in mid-June (although, as the name indicates, the latter races were once rowed in May).

With the establishing of a rowing governing body, Cambridge University BC, the organisation sent a challenge to Oxford University on 20 February 1829 which read: 'The University of Cambridge hereby challenge the University of Oxford to row a match at or near London each in an 8 oared boat during the ensuing Easter vacation'. Oxford accepted the challenge, but only if the race could be conducted in June or beginning of July.

On 10 June, an estimated 20,000 people gathered in Henley-on-Thames to watch the race. This is a remarkable figure as there was not yet a railway to bring all these spectators to the small market town;

they could only travel by horse or horse and carriage or on foot. The race was rowed from Hambleden Lock to Henley Bridge and was won by Oxford. Despite the successful start of the Boat Race, it took seven years before the next race between the universities took place, in June 1836, now between Westminster and Putney on the River Thames – and this time Cambridge won.

Although the Boat Race between Oxford and Cambridge moved to the Thames in London, the town of Henley-on-Thames saw boat races take place on the Henley Reach after 1829. In March 1839, Captain Edmund Gardiner proposed at a public meeting that the town should organise an annual regatta for amateurs 'under judicious and respectable management, [which] would not only be productive of the most beneficial results to the town of Henley, but from its peculiar attractions would also be a source of amusement and gratification to the neighbourhood, and the public in general' (a quote in rowing historian Christopher Dodd's book *Henley Royal Regatta*; 1981). The regatta proved to be a great success and expanded in days from one day in 1839, two days in 1840 and three days in 1886 (and four days in 1906 and five days in 1986).

"The Oxford & Cambridge Rowing Match at Henley on Thames" by landscape painter William Havell.

Already early on, boat racing was an important and popular activity at Cambridge, which was shown in *The Cambridge Review.* During Michaelmas term, as the autumn term is called at Cambridge University, the magazine published reports from the colleges' boat clubs about their 'tubbing', which was done in a 'tub-pair'. This boat type was a wide, clinker-built, inrigged or half-outrigged gig, which would take two oarsmen on fixed or moving seats and their coach, who sat in the stern facing both oarsmen and acting as coxswain. The boat clubs used these 'tubs' to take out the freshmen for outings to be able to evaluate whether there were any promising 'oars' among them. Tubbing was also used by the coach to polish a particular oarsman's technique or blade work, or over-all watermanship. The tub was, in the words of G. O. Nickalls and P. C. Mallam, 'the nursery of oarsmen'.

In 1881, to help the novice oarsmen, Rudolph 'Rudie' Chamber Lehmann, a coach and well-known authority on rowing, who had studied at Cambridge, had published a seven-page booklet called *Tubbing, hints for the coaching of freshmen in tub pairs (fixed seats).* Some years before Hunting Howell arrived at Cambridge, Lehmann had painted a somewhat romantic picture of being an aspiring rowing freshman at Cambridge in *The English Illustrated Magazine.* In the article "Rowing at Cambridge" (1890), he wrote:

Before entering upon the serious business of life as a freshman at Cambridge, the youth who is subsequently to become an oar will in probability have fired his imagination by reading of historical prowess of past generations of University oars and of great deeds of the present. [John] Goldie who turned the tide of defeat, the Closes [William, John and James], [H. E.] Rhodes, [Charles] Gurdon, [T. E.] Hockin, [Freddie] Pitman the gallantest of strokes, and [Stanley] Muttlebury the mighty President of to-day are the heroes whom he worships, and to whose imitation he proposes to devote himself. A vision of a light blue coat and cap flits before his mind, he sees himself in fancy wresting a fiercely contested victory from the clutches of Oxford, and cheered and feted by a countless throng of his admirers. With these ideas he becomes as a freshman a member of his College Boat Club, and adds his name to the 'tubbing list'.

A young Rudie Lehmann around the time his article "Rowing at Cambridge" was published in *The English Illustrated Magazine* in 1890.

It was very likely that Howell began tubbing at the Hall shortly after he arrived at Cambridge at Michaelmas term in 1894. With his 6 ft. 5 in. and 12 st. 8 lb. (196 cm and 79.8 kg), and his long, strong arms, which gave him an enormous reach, he had every chance to succeed at the oar. He was described as having a friendly, oval face with a low forehead, blue eyes, Roman nose, medium mouth, round chin and dark hair: Hunting Howell must have been a striking fellow to watch in a boat out on the river.

CHAPTER 2
1895: 'The Hall, the Hall,
I Bawl the Hall'

In 1895, the Lent Races had to be cancelled due to the Cam being frozen for seven weeks – it was even possible to skate from Cambridge to Ely. Five men from the Hall, including the cox Francis C. Begg, who was the only 'Old Blue' from the previous year, were in the losing Cambridge crew in the Boat Race against Oxford on 30 March.

Because of the light blue coloured trim Cambridge had on their white jerseys, they came to be named the 'Light Blues', while Oxford, with a dark blue trim on their jerseys, were the 'Dark Blues'.

The Hall had their first races at the May Races, in which their first eight easily defended the Head from the previous year. There were three new members in the crew, among them Hunting Howell in the six seat, which is one of the positions where the largest and strongest men ended up, the boat's 'engine room'.

The professional oarsman Bill East, who would become Howell's sculling coach, wrote in his *Rowing and Sculling* (1904), that the man in the six seat 'must be both a powerful and stylish rower. On his side of the boat he comes next to stroke, and must be able to detect and follow him in every slightest change. A heavy weight does well at this post'.

Encouraged by their newly won Headship in the May Races, Trinity Hall decided to go for the Grand Challenge Cup at Henley Royal Regatta that summer. 'The Grand' was, and is, the most prominent of the events for first-class eights at Henley. The college also entered a four for the Visitors' Challenge Cup.

This was far fewer crews than the Hall's glory year of 1887 at Henley, the boat club's *annus mirabilis*. Of course, none of them had been around to see the races then – with one exception. One man among the Hall men had actually been at Henley that year, the Trinity Hall BC coach Henry Tudor Trevor-Jones. He had despatched the telegrams from Henley to inform the college about the Hall's victories, Julian Ebsworth writes in his article "A Boat Club Saga" in the wonderful book *The Hidden Hall – Portrait of a College* (2004). These telegrams still hang on a wall at the college.

Two prominent Hall oarsmen that year were Reginald McKenna and Charles J. Bristowe, who both rowed in the winning Cambridge Blue boat (Bristowe also in 1886). As a curiosity, the previous spring, in 1886, before the May Races, the Hall crews had been coached by an oarsman from Jesus College by the name of Steve Fairbairn, the famous Cambridge coach-to-be of the 1920s and 1930s, who was a winning 1887 Blue, too.

The 1887 Henley Royal Regatta had been a remarkable regatta for Cambridge, as the university had won all the events. The Hall won the Grand Challenge Cup for eight-oars, the Ladies' Challenge Plate for eight-oars, the Thames Challenge Cup for eight-oars, the Stewards' Challenge Cup for four-oars and the Visitors' Challenge Cup for four-oars. Pembroke College had taken the Wyfold Challenge Cup for four-oars, Third Trinity's Charles Barclay and Stanley 'Muttle' Muttlebury won the Silver Goblets Cup for pair-oars. James C. Gardner of Emmanuel College crossed the finish line ahead of Guy Nickalls of Magdalen College, Oxford, in the Diamond Challenge Sculls. In the race, the unfortunate Nickalls had crashed into a boating party that had floated out onto the course in front of him because there were no booms stopping spectator boats from interfering with the racing crews.

A correspondent for a newspaper wrote about the Hall:

Trinity Hall as a whole have given the rowing world a wonderful lesson of what combining swing with leg-work and a comfortable, though not beautiful, style can do [...] But a good style of rowing will not win races; there is one other essential in which we must say the Hall stands facile princeps, and that is keenness. Any outsider must be struck with the extra vigour of the general Trinity Hall coach; no other boat gets so much abuse as a Hall boat, and yet the men seem to like it. Is it not chiefly because all successful colleges have a very deep spirit of esprit de corps and unselfish love of the club that they are so successful?

The Hall coach Henry Trevor-Jones – known to the oarsmen as just 'T-J' – was a real character. In 1875, at the age of 20, he came up to Trinity Hall and rowed in some successful second and third boats, but he never made it to a Hall's first boat. After he had taken an MA degree in 1882, Trevor-Jones tutored pupils at his home at 3 Trinity Street. Henry Bond wrote in *A History of the Trinity Hall Boat Club* (1930) that Trevor-Jones 'every afternoon for many years was to be found at the river tubbing men and coaching crews from the back of an ancient white horse, called Sultan, popularly supposed to be nearly as old as his rider'. Trevor-Jones coached many Hall crews successfully, but he was less victorious coaching any Light Blue boats.

Trevor-Jones had his 'weaknesses', Bond mentioned in his book, as he 'had strong prejudices against certain persons and certain boat clubs, and these it was next to impossible to remove, with the result that there were now and then difficulties between the Hall and other clubs'. But not only would problems arise with other clubs, as the Hall coach 'sometimes also failed to hit it off with the Hall boat captains, and the coaching of the crews suffered in consequence'.

In 1895, Trevor-Jones's name appeared in a small book of poetry, *Horace at Cambridge*, written by Owen Seaman, who had been admitted to Clare College, Cambridge, in 1880. These light verses by Seaman, who was regarded as a 'literary godson' of Rudie Lehmann, had earlier been published in *The Granta*, a magazine founded by students in 1889 and with Lehmann as its first editor.

Seaman's "Of those that go down to the River" was a humorous verse, which, very much like Lehmann's article in *The English Illustrated Magazine* five years earlier, gave the freshmen a taste of what they could expect if they were drawn to the river. The five last stanzas read:

A time before booms were placed on the regatta course — "Look Ahead, Sir! Reminiscence of Henley Regatta", a print from 1880 showing how crowded the river could be during the regatta.

Full often, rowing like an ox,
On you the curses of your cox,
Falling like blasts of some Tyrrhenian trumpet,
Will rend the horror-stricken air
With language fit to curl the hair
That clusters nicely round the fair
Crest of your crumpet.

Then will you at your rigid thwart
Restrain the apposite retort
And like the parrot merely think profanely,
The while your heavy head you wag
Panting as pants the hunted stag,
And wear your 'Pontius' to a rag,
Sliding inanely.

Perchance you will mislay your oar,
When quickening to forty-four,
And learn a little jargon from your skipper;
Or get an unexpected spank
Straight in the centre of your flank
From some inordinately rank
Holiday-tripper.

Those coaches you shall come to know,
That trot with caution to and fro
And wish their knowledge of the chase were larger;
Your valour shall divert the way
Of Nestor-Jones's (1) blinkered grey,
And draw a compliment from J.
B. (2) on his charger.

Eventually you will land
Triumphant after trials, and
Talk frankly like a father from the saddle
You have the makings of a tar,
And should, with fortune, travel far;

Meanwhile you might get forward. Are
You ready? Paddle!"

'Nestor-Jones' was of course Trevor-Jones, described by Seaman in a footnote as the 'popular and perpetual coach of Trinity Hall'. In a second footnote Seaman wrote that 'J.B.' was 'J. B. Close, President of the C.U.B.C., 1894-5' which demands an explanation. James B. Close rowed in three winning Cambridge crews in 1872, 1873 and 1874. The latter year, he was president of Cambridge University BC. For the 1895 Light Blue crew, Close was elected president again in April 1894 because he lived in Cambridge, but he did not row in the 1895 Boat Race. It was an attempt to unite the different colleges' boat clubs. W. W. R. Ball wrote in *A History of The First Trinity Boat Club* (1908): 'The constitution of the [1894 Light Blue] crew and its style of rowing were again bitterly criticized in Cambridge, and at any rate the result did not justify the style. An unpleasant controversy ensued', so Close was elected president. With a non-rowing president, the cox Francis Begg undertook the captaincy of the crew.

James B. Close's older brother, John B., also rowed for Cambridge and earned his Blue in 1871 and 1872, and his younger brother, William B., earned his Blue in 1875, 1876 (president) and 1877.

In 1894, Owen Seaman had his first contribution published in *Punch* and in 1897 he joined the staff at 'The Table' (the senior staff of *Punch* met around a table at a restaurant once every week for lunch to discuss the content for the following week's issue). Between 1906 and 1932 Seaman was the editor of the magazine. In a second edition of *Horace at Cambridge*, which was published in 1902, the stanza in which Trevor-Jones and Close were mentioned was removed.

Another contributor to *Punch* was Joseph Ashby-Sterry, an artist and versifier who is still remembered for some poems about Henley. About the 1886 regatta in Henley, he jestingly wrote:

I don't care, you know, a bit how they row,
Nor mind about smartness of feather;
If steering is bad, I'm not at all sad,
Nor care if they all swing together!
Oh why do they shout and make such a rout,

When one boat another one chases?
'Tis really too hot to bawl, is it not?
Or bore oneself over the Races!
I don't care a rap for the Races! –
Mid all the Regatta embraces –
I'm that sort of chap, I don't care a rap,
A rap or a snap for the Races!

From "A Regatta Rhyme (On board the 'Athena', Henley-on-Thames)", published in *Punch* on 10 July 1886.

———————————————————————

The 1895 Henley Royal Regatta was rowed between 9 and 11 July, a Tuesday, Wednesday and Thursday, three hot days with occasionally strong winds on the first day. To commemorate that his sons Guy and Vivian had won the pair-oared event, the Silver Goblets, either together or with others for the fifth time, Tom Nickalls presented a new challenge cup, which still today is called The Silver Goblets and Nickalls' Challenge Cup. At the regatta, the Nickalls brothers, who rowed for the London RC, easily won the cup, in the final beating W. Broughton and S. Muttlebury of Thames RC.

Despite some interesting races, the year 1895 has gone down in the history of Henley Royal Regatta for one particular race, a 'scandal' that involved Leander Club and Cornell University, the first American eight to compete in the Grand Challenge Cup.

In 1894, Cornell University in Ithaca, New York State, decided to investigate if their best eight was welcome to race in England. A Cornell man, Horatio S. White, who was in Europe for a year, rapidly went to England to talk to 'the leading rowing authorities of both Oxford and Cambridge University'. As it was impossible to get together an English university crew during the summer, when the Cornell eight wanted to come, the question went to the Henley Stewards if it was possible for Cornell to race in the Grand at Henley, Horatio S. White wrote in an article in *The Cornell Magazine* in December 1894. The Henley Stewards accepted the Americans' application.

White's ten-and-a-half-page article leaves a remarkable piece of information about the regatta for the readers of *The Cornell Maga-*

zine and for us today. He told the readers which cruising lines to take across the Atlantic, which cities to visit on the way to Henley-on-Thames, which cups there were at the regatta and when they were established. He wrote a good description of the course, published the full 18-point laws of boat racing observed at the regatta, what a visitor would see along the towpath (the 'cheap and light amusements are present, the fakir, the tumbler, the hawker, the masked quartette, and the fake Ethiopian's minstrel strains') and how 'prominent Englishmen' welcomed the presence of a Cornell crew at Henley – 'perhaps the most welcome utterance of this sort to Cornellians would be the words of "Tom" Hughes [author of the famous books *Tom Brown's School Days* (1857) and *Tom Brown at Oxford* (1861)]'.

In his article, White also mentioned some previous foreigners racing at Henley, among them Charles Psotta, a graduate of Cornell, who was the 1888 U.S. amateur champion in the single sculls, who sculled in the Diamonds twice, in 1889 and 1890. In 1889, Psotta, rowing for New York Athletic Club, was beaten in the final by Guy Nickalls, who only had a row-over to reach the final. The following year, the American managed to warm many hearts in his first heat of the Diamonds at Henley. This is how the story goes in the words of Guy Nickalls:

> In the Diamonds the first heat was between C. J. Psotta, rowing under the colours of the Schuykill Navy Club, Philadelphia, and G. E. B. Kennedy [Kingston RC]. Kennedy bet Psotta twenty-five pounds level money that he would beat him. After a dozen strokes or so Kennedy caught a crab, broke the gate of his swivel, and went overboard. Psotta might, if he wished, have paddled over and claimed his twenty-five pounds and the race and got both; but no, he was too good a sportsman, he stopped, backed down to the start, and waited till Kennedy got ashore, fixed up his swivel, and started again. Eventually Psotta was beaten, somewhat easily this time.

Then, White mentioned in his article the Cornell four that raced in the Stewards' in 1881. In a three-boat heat, together with Thames RC and the London RC, and after a restart due to a foul between the American crew and the London RC, Cornell led at the start, but was soon overpowered by both the English crews.

After their Henley race, the Cornellians went to race at a regatta in Vienna. The American stroke, J. N. D. Shinkel, disgraced himself by pretending to faint in the middle of the race, when his boat was well in the lead. The rest of the crew accused him for having thrown the race, which proved to be true. Newspapers all over Europe, including the English, wrote about this scandal.

By the time of the Cornellians visit to Henley in 1895, many Americans – non-rowers, that is – were drawn to England and to Henley Royal Regatta. To many of these visitors, the regatta was more a social event than a sport competition. One of the reasons for this was that gossip columnists in American newspapers and magazines fed their readers with stories of American upper-class ladies who had married into the English aristocracy and were holding garden parties and social soirees in their new country. Ever since the regatta in Henley had received its Royal patronage in 1851, it had become an event which was visited by the upper-classes which led to further Americans patronizing the regatta, and therefore 'every year at Henley Regatta the number of houseboats which fly the Stars and Stripes increases', Henry Wellington Wack wrote in *In Thamesland*, a book published in 1906 (a quote in the book *Victorians on the Thames* by R. R. Bolland, 1974).

The first foreign amateur crew racing in England was a Harvard coxed four, which had challenged Oxford for a race between Putney and Mortlake on the Thames in August 1869 (Oxford won). The first 'overseas' competitor at Henley was also from America, E. Smith of Atlanta RC, New York, who entered for the Diamonds in 1872. His entry was followed by 'an invasion' for the 1878 regatta, Gilbert C. Bourne wrote in *Memories of an Eton Wet-Bob of the Seventies* (1933), when there were two American entries for the Diamonds, G. W. Lee of New Jersey and G. Lee of Boston, and two fours, the Shoe-wae-cae-mette BC of Monroe, Michigan, for the Stewards' and Columbia College for both the Stewards' and Visitors'.

The Henley Stewards would later question the amateur status of the French Canadian lumberjacks in the Shoe-wae-cae-mette BC crew and G. W. Lee, which made the rowing journalist and historian Richard Burnell write in one of his history books on the regatta, 'Unhappily the first foreign invasion of Henley had a sour aftermath', or,

"Henley Royal Regatta" by Lucien Davis.

as Christopher Dodd puts it in *The Story of World Rowing* (1992), 'It was hard to be French, Canadian and a gentleman in 1878'. This raises the question of what an 'overseas' or 'foreign' crew actually meant? Already in 1870, Henley Royal Regatta saw the first appearance of a club from Ireland. Rowing historian Greg Denieffe writes:

Trinity College, Dublin became not only the first Irish entry but also the first from overseas, albeit at that time not a foreign entry. They entered for the Grand, Ladies', Stewards', Visitors', Wyfolds, Goblets and Diamonds but thinking better of it and having only nine men to man the boats, they withdrew from the Stewards' and the Wyfolds. At the end of the regatta, Ireland recorded its first victory, in the Visitors', which in 1870 was still an event for coxed fours.

In early June 1895, when it was time for the Cornell crew to leave Ithaca for Henley, the whole town, including a band and military troops, showed up to escort the young American oarsmen, who were all dressed up in their new lounging suits, to the railway station. There a special train took them to New York where the steamer SS *Paris* sailed them across the Atlantic Ocean to Southampton, England, together with 1,178 other passengers.

Along with the Cornell crew aboard *Paris* was their coach, Charles Courtney, who had once been one of America's best scullers. Starting out as an amateur sculling champion with eighty-eight victories – out of eighty-eight races – Courtney entered into the all too often shady business of a professional sculler, racing for wages. His most famous races as a professional were in 1878, 1879 and 1880 when he three times lost to Ned Hanlan of Toronto, Canada. Later in 1880, the Canadian would become the world professional sculling champion, beating the holder Ned Trickett of Sydney, Australia. In 1883, Courtney coached the Cornell crews for a short while, and later came back to train the university's crews full-time in 1885.

As a coach Courtney was a strict disciplinarian, which he proved during the voyage to England. His oarsmen were not allowed to fraternise with any of the other passengers, especially not the young ladies. The American oarsmen's isolation continued when they arrived at Henley, where they were not to socialise with the spectators

Charles Courtney, in the beginning of the 1880s.

or the other competitors. Courtney also avoided talking to the other coaches at the regatta.

His crew rowed with a fast, short stroke and with no body swing that seemed unusual on these waters. Rudie Lehmann, who in 1895 was captain of Leander and had an interest in his club's opponents, left an account of a conversation he had on the towpath with 46-year-old Courtney, who sounded very ill-tempered. Lehmann wrote in *The Complete Oarsman* (1908):

> They [Cornell's crew] had several peculiarities which still remain in the minds of those who saw their rowing. The chief of these was that of the oarsmen, just before attaining the limit of their reach, turned their blades completely over from the feather so that the concave side lay for a moment over the water. I asked their coach [Charles Courtney] the reason for this, but he gave me none. All he said was that the men were not performing the movement as he wished it performed, and he led me to infer that he looked on it with disapproval. My own impression is that he imagined that by this movement they were able to seize the water an inch or two further back, and with greater cleanness. It appears to me, however, to be in the result a pure waste of energy.

Leander had had a four-year-run winning the Grand, and Charles W. Kent, the stroke of the Leander boat those years, was expecting to triumph for the fifth time in the 1895 Grand. In the first heat, the Hall defeated the London RC without any problems, leading at Fawley (which more or less is the half-way point of the course) and crossing the finish line two boat lengths ahead. The members of the Hall crew were: bow Theodore B. Hope, 2 John A. Bott, 3 William J. Fernie, 4 Frederick C. Stewart, 5 William A. Bieber, 6 B. Hunting Howell, 7 Adam S. Bell, stroke David A. Wauchope and cox Thomas R. Paget-Tomlinson. In the second heat Eton beat Thames RC by slightly more than a length.

In the third heat Leander was to row against Cornell. At the start, the Leander crew looked comfortable at the stake boat on the Berks (Berkshire) side. There was a wind blowing off the Bucks (Buckinghamshire) side and when the umpire, Colonel Frank Willan, called out: 'Are you ready', some members of the English crew called: 'No!' Colonel Willan seemed not to have heard this and sent the crews off. The Americans started immediately, while a few oarsmen in the Leander crew took a stroke or two, and then stopped, expecting the umpire to call back Cornell for a restart. Willan, however, thought that

In the 17 January 1895 issue of the magazine *Vanity Fair*, Rudie Lehmann was depicted by 'SPY', pseudonym for the portrait artist and caricaturist Leslie Ward.

Leander had made a bad start and did not call back the Americans, who at one point eased off on their strokes to see if Willan would stop the race. But he waved at the Americans to continue, which they did. The umpire launch followed Cornell over the course and gave them the victory when they crossed the finish line, with Leander still sitting at the stake boat at the start.

According to American newspapers, 5,000 American spectators had found their way to Henley that day to cheer on Cornell. At first, the Cornell crew was met with applaudes coming down the course, but when it was clear that Leander did not even start, which, as a matter of fact, was the verdict Colonel Willan gave the umpire at the finish line, this became an extremely unpopular victory for the young Americans. The English part of the large Henley crowd was outraged, and the English papers accused the Americans of unsportsmanlike behaviour as they did not stop rowing when they saw that Leander did not start. For the home crews it had been a somewhat unwritten Henley rule for a boat which was ahead of another boat to stop if the crew saw that their opponents were in trouble, catching a bad crab or being interfered with a punt or 'pleasure boat'. Of course, the Cornellians, who were abroad for the first time in their lives, knew nothing about this, and none of them seemed to have heard about Psotta's gentleman gesture five years earlier.

Coach Courtney had taken ill that day and was not on board the umpire's launch to stop his oarsmen, had he wanted to. Aboard the launch were the American Ambassador Thomas F. Bayard and some American journalists, which might have been the reason why Willan was unwilling to stop the race.

How the race was conducted and its outcome just added to the already poor reputation of the isolated Americans and their professional coach who wanted to win the race at all costs, not giving Leander a fair chance, or so it was expressed in the English press. *The New York Times* mentioned the day after the race (on 10 July) that it was an 'unfortunate heat'. On another note, the paper also wrote that there were many beautiful decorated houseboats along the course, among them *Rouge-et-Noir*, which had on board American dignitaries like the staff from the American Embassy, including Secretary Teddy Roosevelt, but also 'F. H. Howell and B. Howell of New York'.

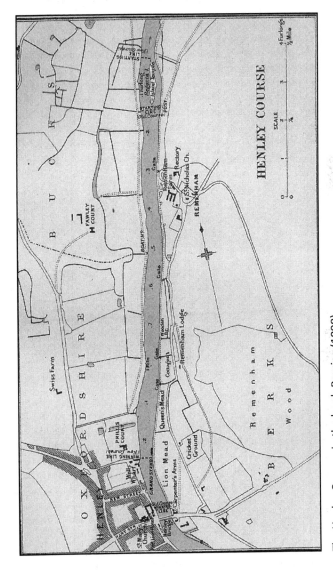

The Henley Course, in the book *Rowing* (1898).

The defeat of Cornell University in the fifth heat for the 1895 Grand Challenge Cup according to the artist Sydney P. Hall in *The Graphic*, 20 July 1895. About this race, the paper wrote: 'At first the Americans led by a few feet, and at the half-mile mark were half a length in front; but soon after that the Cambridge began to overhaul them. The fast stroke of the Cornell crew had told heavily on the men, and Trinity Hall went in front at the mile post. Opposite the Ishmian Club the Americans were being rapidly left behind, and at the Grand Stand were so exhausted as to be scarcely able to pull their oars through the water.'

The day after the 'unfortunate heat', 'English justice was done', Christopher Dodd writes in his *Henley Royal Regatta*. The Hall met Cornell in the semifinal and the Cambridge college crew 'pulled past Cornell at the Mile Post and got a verdict of "Easily" after the American crew broke up in disarray and exhaustion by the time they reached Phyllis Court'. The Hall crew's victory was greeted with delight among the English spectators, and in the evening the town was very boisterous with, Richard Burnell writes in *Henley Regatta: A History* (1957), 'the all-too-obvious, distortion of the battle-cry, "Cornell, Cornell, I yell Cornell", and the newly coined counter-cry of "The Hall, the Hall, I bawl the Hall"'.

It is not known how Howell felt being a member of a crew that totally crushed his countrymen in this way.

In the final race of the Grand, the Hall raced New College, after the Oxford crew had defeated Eton in an earlier heat. The race between the Hall and New College was grand. From start to finish, the crews alternated leading and there was never more than a half-length between the boats. At the end, the Cambridge boat managed to hold on to a slight lead and won by a third of a length.

The Hall also raced in the Visitors', where in the first heat, Hope, Howell, Bieber and Bell, beat First Trinity, Cambridge. In the final, they were defeated by Trinity College, Oxford. This race was the same day as the Hall's race in the Grand, so Howell and his fellow oarsmen still had that race in their legs.

Before the Cornell crew left England for America, they published a statement:

In the view of the discussion over the action of the Cornell crew in Tuesday's race, we believe the position of the Cornell crew in the matter should be clearly defined. The umpire, as we interpret the rules of racing, has entire control of a race after it has been started, and to disregard his command is sufficient reason to disqualify a crew. On Tuesday the usual question, 'Are you ready?' was asked, and as no negative reply was heard by the umpire from either crew, the word 'Go' was given. Cornell started and Leander also drew away from the post. We soon discovered that Leander had stopped rowing, but the umpire did not recall us, nor did he in any way indicate his desire to have us return. Had he done so, we would have stopped at any point on the course. He followed us to the finish, and awarded us the heat.

Under the rules governing racing as we understand them, had Cornell not rowed over the course, we would have been liable to disqualification from entry into any subsequent heat, and thereby debarred from further competition for the Grand Challenge contest. No one can regret the outcome of this lamentable affair more than the members of the Cornell crew. They certainly did not come to England to claim a race from Leander or any other crew by default.

The crew has never authorized any statement to the effect that Cornell would not consider a proposition for another trail between Leander and ourselves. However, we did not feel at liberty to suggest a

The 1895 Cornell crew: cox F. D. Colson, stroke S. Hall, 7 C. A. Louis, 6 S. J. Dyer, 5 T. F. Fennell, 4 F. W. Freeborn (captain), 3 E. C. Hager, 2 E. O. Spillman and bow M. W. Roe.

contest until after the subsequent heats had been decided. It certainly would have been premature on the part of Cornell to take any action in the matter before the result of the subsequent heat in which Cornell was to row, since Leander would undoubtedly not care to row us had we been defeated by another crew. So far as Cornell is concerned in connection with the Grand Challenge Cup, we acknowledge our defeat after a hard race with Trinity Hall. We have no excuses to offer; we were fairly beaten, and we take this opportunity to express our sincere thanks to the English public for the many courtesies extended to us during our five weeks' sojourn in their country.

[signed] *Freeborn*

Unfortunately, this explanation by the American oarsmen, for what it was worth, would very soon be forgotten. Instead, the Henley Stewards, the English rowing journalists, the English rowing establishment and the English Henley crowd for years to come would look at crews from America with suspicion.

When the Hall four met First Trinity again in the first heat of the Light Fours race at the Michaelmas term, the Hall crew thought that First Trinity would be an easy victory. But First Trinity beat them by a few feet.

Later that autumn, Adam Bell won the Colquhoun Sculls, which was a prize established in 1837 at Cambridge University by Patrick Colquhoun, the same year he won the Wingfield Sculls. The latter prize, also known as the 'Silver Sculls' in the early days, had been presented in 1830 by Henry C. Wingfield for amateurs as a sculling championship of the Thames and Great Britain. The first championship race for professional scullers took place the following year, also on the Thames. While the race for the professionals came to be fairly well known, it is, as rowing historian Tim Koch puts it, 'strange that an event that carries the grandiose titles of "The British Amateur Sculling Championship and Championship of the Thames" should be so obscure, even within the sport of rowing and sculling'.

In December 1895, Howell was in the crew that won the 'Trial eights'. This event was, and still is, when the coaches gathered all the rowing talents from the university's boat clubs for practice and to test their performance and skills to be able to form two eights that will race against each other. The Trials gave the coaches a good idea of how the sixteen oarsmen and the two coxes would handle mental endurance and the stress to row a side-by-side race. Depending on who was still in residence, the Trial eights were composed of a mix of freshmen and oarsmen who did not make the Blue boat the previous time. During training in the eights a few 'old oars' were also thrown in. Of course, who would ultimately race in the Blue boat all depended on how the individual oarsmen improved and developed from the Trials in December to the Boat Race in early spring. The Cambridge Trial eights were rowed at Ely, north-north-east of Cambridge, where the broader waters of the Great Ouse allowed side-by-side races.

CHAPTER 3
1896: A New River Adventure

Although Hunting Howell had rowed in the winning Trial eight in December 1895, he was not picked for the 1896 Light Blue boat. Instead, the Hall was represented by Theodore Hope, William Bieber, Adam Bell, William Fernie, who stroked the boat, and Thomas Paget-Tomlinson, the cox. Cambridge had not won the Boat Race since 1889 and had high hopes to overcome Oxford, but in the end the Dark Blues won with two-fifths of a length.

That spring, Bell was elected President of Cambridge University BC, and he and Fernie easily took the Magdalene Pairs trophy. Thereby, Bell had won every racing event on the Cam. The Hall's first eight won the Head at the May Races – with Howell in the six seat – but it had been a struggle, as most of the members of the crew had been ill the week prior to the races.

The Hall's first eight came to the 1896 Henley Royal Regatta on 7-9 July as the holders of the Grand. In their first heat, the Hall raced against New College, which they had overpowered in a hard race in the previous year's final. This time, however, New College got its revenge and the Hall eight was kicked out after only one race. It did not go better for the Hall's second eight in the Ladies'. It lost to Emmanuel College, Cambridge. The same crews met again in the Thames Challenge Cup after the Hall had beaten Kingston RC. Again, Emmanuel proved to be the stronger crew. Emmanuel eventually won the Thames Cup by beating the French crew from Societé d'Encouragment du Sport Nautique of Paris in the final.

During Michaelmas term, in October 1896, Hunting Howell began a new river adventure: sculling. What was previously said about Howell's physique – he was strong and his long arms gave him a tremendous reach – also made him a good sculler, alhough, as beginners in a single scull can verify, it is not an easy boat to master. Howell capsized three times on the first day of practice, he later told a reporter. This indicates that he did not go about the usual way of learning how to scull. Normally a novice would begin his first attempts in a sturdy boat, for example a fixed-seat inrigged gig, or maybe a half-outrigged boat. Then, when the beginner was comfortable sculling in this boat type, he would try a 'whiff', which was a lighter, clinker-built, outrigged boat. Maybe Howell started out in this kind of boat, or even a more narrow shell, or why else would he have flipped around?

In a book published a couple of years after Howell began to scull, *Rowing* (1898) by R. P. P. Rowe and C. M. Pitman, there was some helpful advice for the rower who wanted to become a sculler. The authors' fifth recommendation stated: 'Make your first attempt in the summer, when the water is warm and pleasant to swim in', which Howell obviously did not follow. Let us hope that he at least followed Rowe and Pitman's sixth bit of advice: 'If you upset in the Cam, send your clothes to the wash'.

Some weeks later, on Tuesday 17 November, Howell was ready to take part in the Colquhoun Sculls, the Cambridge University Sculling Championships. In the final, he met Harold Gould of First Trinity. A short report published in *The Times* the following day informed that despite 'dull weather' a fairly large crowd had gathered to watch the race on the Cam. The newspaper wrote:

Advice for a novice sculler: 'Make your first attempt in the summer, when the water is warm and pleasant to swim in'.

The issue was between H. U. Gould, First Trinity, and B. H. Howell, Trinity Hall. Although the latter had on Monday won his heat in 8 sec. faster time than Gould, the First Trinity man was a slight favourite, and this was justified by the result. Gould at once commenced to gain, and he held an advantage of 30 yards at Grassy Corner. This was increased to 40 yards at Ditton Corner. Upon entering the straight in Long Reach Howell responded gamely to the calls of his coach and recovered a lot of his lost distance. His effort, however, proved futile, Gould winning a most exciting struggle by two yards, amid great cheering on the part of his fellow collegians. Time 8 min. 30 sec. The winner [...] did not take up sculling until last summer, whilst Howell, who comes from New York, first made acquaintance with sculling a boat a fortnight ago [sic].

Towards the end of Michaelmas term, oarsmen from the different colleges' boat clubs, including Howell and some of his fellow comrades from the Hall, practiced to try to make it into the two Trial eights. On 26 November 1896, *The Cambridge Review* published an article about the sixteen oarsmen and two coxes who made it into the two eights. The first boat had the following crew: bow Henry E. H. Oakeley (Jesus), 2 John E. Payne (Peterhouse), 3 George E. P. Cave-Moyles (Caius), 4 Harold G. Brown (First Trinity), 5 Stephen J. Selwyn (Third Trinity), 6 Gerard A. Crane (First Trinity), 7 Sydney V. Pearson (Emmanuel), stroke Charles M. Steele (Trinity Hall) and cox William H. G. Woodroffe (Emmanuel). In the second boat rowed: bow David E. Campbell-Muir (Trinity Hall), 2 James S. Munro-Sutherland (Jesus), 3 Raymond B. Etherington-Smith (First Trinity), 4 Peter L. May (Lady Margaret), 5 B. Hunting Howell (Trinity Hall), 6 Clive R. Pattison-Muir (Caius), 7 Gerald T. Bullard (Trinity Hall), stroke Claude J. D. Goldie (Third Trinity) and cox Francis E. Foster (Trinity Hall).

Although the author of the article in *The Cambridge Review* thought that the oarsmen of the two eights were 'rather above average', his criticism of most of them was severe. He wrote that number seven in the first boat 'should try to sit up more and carry his shoulder back at the finish', while number six 'seems to have no control over his slide' and number five 'is trying to do much work, and sacrificing all body form in consequence'. Also number three had problems with his slide, 'his body swing is long but not in unison with his slide'. About number two, the writer wrote that he 'has apparently taught himself the first principles of rowing or has at any rate lacked good coaching' and that bow 'makes no use whatever of his outside hand'.

The second Cambridge Trial eight also received tough criticisms: the stroke 'is swinging rather out of the boat, and finish by turning his wrists instead of dropping them from the elbow'. Number seven 'is one of the hardest workers, but he kicks his slide away badly at times and does not row his hands right on to his chest'. Number six was 'inclined to rush his slide up and hang over the stretcher', while four seemed to be just plain 'poor'. Number three 'would be very fair if he did not over-reach so badly, and rush his slide up'. Two's 'chief fault is that he tries to knock his front stop off'. The bow 'is rowing very much below his best form. When he likes he can row well, but at present he is lying back in the bottom of the boat long after his blade is out of the water, and consequently is always half a stroke late on the rest of the crew'.

Hunting Howell rowed in the second boat on bow side as number five and about Howell, the author wrote that he 'is not rowing up to his best form. He has been sculling of late, which seems to have upset him rather and that with a change of sides and absence from bad health makes it scarcely fair to criticize him too severely. He is a very hard worker'. On the Trial eights race day, on 5 December, the American proved to be a hard worker, indeed, as it was his boat that won.

Of course, it was impossible for the author of the article to see into the future, but we, who have the results and record books at hand, can amuse ourselves with the knowledge that twelve years later, the oarsman in the three seat in the second Trial eight, Raymond Etherington-Smith, by his friends called 'Ethel', would become a 1908 Olympic gold medallist in the eights at Henley, rowing with the 'Old Crocks' of Leander Club.

There is a wonderful photograph from December 1896 showing Hunting Howell and the other fifteen oarsmen and two coxes in their 'Trial caps', a cap given to the oarsmen and coxes who made it into the two Trial eights. In the picture are also some 'old oars' and the Trinity Hall coach Henry Trevor-Jones on his old horse, Sultan. The 'old' Hall oarsmen, including Trevor-Jones, wear the distinguished

Sixteen oarsmen and two coxes proudly wearing their 'Trial caps' for the Cambridge Trial eights race on 5 December 1896. Back row, left to right: (unidentified), C. R. Pattison-Muir (Caius), S. V. Pearson (Emmanuel), Sultan (the horse), D. E. Campbell-Muir (Trinity Hall), coach H. T. Trevor-Jones (on the horse; although at times a difficult man, 'T-J' was a devoted coach for the Hall), (unidentified), J. E. Payne (Peterhouse), H. E. Oakeley (Jesus) and G. A. Crane (First Trinity). Front row, left to right: G. T. Bullard (Trinity Hall), B. H. Howell (Trinity Hall), C. M. Steele (Trinity Hall), (unidentified: 'old oar'?), A. S Bell (old oar, Trinity Hall), W J. Fernie (old oar, Trinity Hall), C. D. J. Goldie (Third Trinity), (unidentified), R. B. Etherington-Smith (First Trinity) and H. G. Brown (First Trinity). Sitting in the front, left to right: W. H. G. Woodroffe (Emmanuel), P. Cave-Moyles (Caius) and F. E. Foster (Trinity Hall).

black and white tartan-patterned Hall cap and some of the Hall oarsmen also wear the college scarf.

It is interesting to see who is not in the photograph. One oarsman, who had not rowed for Cambridge before, did not have to row in the Trials eights to get a seat in the 1897 Light Blue boat, William Dudley-Ward. His reputation as a 'good oar' at Eton had preceded him when he came to Cambridge in the autumn of 1896.

At this time, Cambridge was eager to get 'wet bobs' from Eton. In *Sport and the British: A Modern History* (1989), Richard Holt

Dr. Edmond Warre by 'SPY'.

writes: 'The long domination of the dark over the light blues in the Boat Race of the 1890s was put down to the fact that more Etonians went to Oxford than to Cambridge'. This is true, and looking back in the record books, Cambridge had only one or two Etonians in each crew since their last victory in 1889. For the upcoming race in 1897, besides Dudley-Ward, Bell and Steele had rowed at Eton.

Another Etonian oarsman at Cambridge at this time was the Hon. Rupert Guinness, who also had been admitted in the autumn of 1896, at the age of 22. Guinness had won the Ladies' Challenge Plate for Eton in 1893 and the Diamond Challenge Sculls in 1895 and 1896 (and also the Wingfield Sculls in 1896). At Cambridge, Guinness joined Third Trinity BC in hope of rowing for the university, but because of health problems, he never made an effort to win a seat in a Light Blue boat.

It was the famous rowing coach, housemaster and later headmaster at Eton, Dr. Edmond Warre, who had worked intensely 'to establish Eton as the cornerstone of British rowing' Derek Birley writes in *Sport and the Making of Britain* (1993). At this Dr. Warre had been extremely successful.

Learning to row at Eton meant not only that some rowing freshmen already knew how to handle an oar when they arrived at Oxbridge, but the wet-bobs from Eton, more importantly, were rowing in a uniform style. The coaches of the boat clubs at Cambridge had not agreed on a particular style and therefore each taught rowing in their own way. This problem would be more publicly noticed after the 1897 Boat Race.

CHAPTER 4
1897: Howell Earns his 'Blue'

The weather during January 1897 was tough on the Cam. Some parts of the river were covered with ice, which led to practice being conducted on a few ice-free stretches on the river. Although the crew's practice began on 10 January, Cambridge University BC president Adam Bell came back in residence first on 25 January. Bell started by helping to coach the eight for a couple of days before he claimed his seat at two from Clive Pattison-Muir; previously both Gerald Bullard and James Munro-Sutherland had been tried in this position. Hunting Howell had been absent due to illness, but was at least practicing in a tub-pair, *The Times* wrote on 1 February in an article about the Blue boats' practices. The newspaper continued, 'Fernie is rowing even better than last year, and the Etonian freshman, W. Dudley-Ward, is fully sustaining the high reputation which preceded his arrival at Cambridge. Bieber and Pennington, too, are exhibiting capital form'.

The boat builder Matt Wood of Putney had fitted up one of Cambridge's clinker-built practice boats with nickel rowlocks, while the boat builder Aylings had sent a new set of oars. *The Times* reported that the crew went for an outing in the boat, accompanied by their coaches Stanley Muttlebury and Henry Trevor-Jones. After the crew came back to the dock, the two coaches consulted with president Bell about how to continue the rest of the day's practice, as was the custom at this time when the president was the man in charge of the crew. In the crew that day were: bow Charles Steele, 2 Adam Bell,

3 James Munro-Sutherland, 4 Sydney Pearson, 5 William Bieber, 6 Drury Pennington, 7 William Dudley-Ward, stroke William Fernie and cox Caesar Hawkins.

Also the Dark Blues, who began their practice a week after Cambridge, the newspaper mentioned, had had days of shuffling the crew around in January. Oxford was coached by Douglas 'Ducker' McLean and Gilbert G. Bourne. The Dark Blue crew at the practice was as follows: bow A. Whigworth, 2 Geoffrey O. Edwards, 3 Charles K. Philips, 4 A. O. Dawnson, 5 Ernest Balfour, 6 Russell Carr, 7 Walter Crum (president), stroke Harcourt Gold and cox Horace Pechell.

During the previous years, *The Times* wrote, the Oxford crews had been guests of Rudie Lehmann, who had invited them to his house Fieldhead at Bourne End, northeast of Henley-on-Thames, where there were good rowing waters. However, this year Oxford had to do without Lehmann, who was preparing for his second voyage to America to coach crews at Harvard University.

He had received an invitation in 1896 from his friend Francis Peabody, whom he had rowed with at Cambridge. The rowing at Harvard University was in disorder so Lehmann was offered the opportunity to give Harvard a helping hand, teaching the Crimson crews the proper English stroke. Lehmann arrived in the town of Cambridge, Massachusetts, for the first time in mid-November 1896.

Maybe before he left, or when he came back home to England in December 1896, Lehmann handed in the lyrics for the comic opera *His Majesty, or, The Court of Vingolia* for which rehearsals began in December. The opera opened at the Savoy Theatre in London on 20 February 1897 with a strong cast, with Francis Cowley Burnand as the dramatist and writer (together with Lehmann) and Alexander Mackenzie as the composer. The opera immediately met with disapproval both from the audience and the critics.

Whereas Lehmann was known for his witty writing in the satirical *Punch*, where he had published articles and verses since 1890 – his light verses about rowing gave him the epithet 'The Poet Laureate of Rowing' – it seemed that writing comic opera in the style of Gilbert and Sullivan was not really Lehmann's forté.

On 10 March, probably utterly relieved, Lehmann left England from Liverpool on the SS *Teutonic*, bound for New York, and arrived eight days later. From New York, Lehmann took the midnight train to Boston. According to an interview in *The New York Times* on 19 March 1897, he was especially interested in the race at Poughkeepsie in June, where Harvard was going to race Yale and Cornell in a three-boat competition.

At his first visit, Lehmann had tried to raise interest in an American Henley, which 'would be a great thing for rowing in this country'. Conversely, the American rowing establishment was not interested in an 'American Henley' at this time, as the rowing clubs around the country would not like to travel far for a several-day regatta that offered match races. Yet the question came up again a couple of years later when the writer 'Vigilant', in the magazine *Outing* on 1 April 1899, proposed an American Henley 'entirely collegiate'. He wrote: 'I am of the opinion that if ever this is tried, it will practically revolutionize college rowing, and that it will not take us many years to find a second world's wonder, such as B. H. Howell, and others'.

On 17 February 1897, *The Oxford Magazine* reported that the Cambridge oarsmen and their coach Trevor-Jones had paid a visit to the river where the Oxford crew was training. It had rained heavily before the Light Blues' visit so the towpath was slippery. *The Oxford Magazine* wrote: 'We can only regret that the towpath was in a condition more adapted for nautical evolution than anything else'. When Trevor-Jones stepped into a punt, he slipped so badly that a muscle snapped in his knee and his kneecap was twisted out of place. 'The injury is itself most painful [...] and we can only offer our most sincere sympathy to Mr. Trevor-Jones, and also to the Cambridge crew, on being deprived of so able a coach at an important time in their training', the magazine wrote. Despite the compassionate tone in the article, it is easy to think that the writer had a smirk on his face when he wrote the piece.

After Trevor-Jones's accident, the Cambridge crew's training was left in the hands of president Bell and coach Muttlebury.

Stanley Duff Muttlebury had been one of England's best oarsmen during the late 1880s and rowed for Cambridge in five Light

'Muttle' – 'that brawny king of men'.

Blue crews, becoming a true legend, winning the Boat Race in 1886, 1887, 1888 and 1889, and losing in 1890 – he was the president of Cambridge University BC the last three years. Muttlebury, who was a large, strong man with good manners, was an enormously kind fellow. Affectionately known by the Cambridge rowers as 'Muttle', he not only swept rowing medals and cups at Cambridge, he was equally successful at Henley, though he never won the Grand. Many decades after his active rowing career was over, Muttle was still regarded as 'the greatest oar ever produced by Cambridge'.

About Muttle, Rudie Lehmann wrote in verse:

Muttle at six is 'stylish', so at least The Field reports;
No man has ever worn, I trow, so short a pair of shorts.
His blade sweeps through the water, as he swings his 13.10,
And pulls it all, and more than all, that brawny king of men.

A week before the Boat Race, Sir Charles Dilke, a radical liberal MP (Member of Parliament) who had rowed at Trinity Hall in the 1860s, reported about both Oxford's and Cambridge's training sessions in the article "Two Fine Crews", which was published in *The Saturday Review* on 27 March 1897: 'Oxford is perhaps as fine a University crew as has been seen, and [...] Cambridge is supposed by the public to have weak points'. About the two old Etonians in the Cambridge crew, Sir Charles wrote, 'Seven [Dudley-Ward] and Two [Bell] "get their hands out" Eton fashion; that is, smartly. The rest of the crew are less smart'.

It also seemed that 'the public', whoever this anonymous group might have been, had already picked out a man among the Light Blues to blame for the crew being less perfect. The 'weak point' was Hunting Howell. Nevertheless, Sir Charles did not agree:

> The supposed imperfections of Four [Hunting Howell] [...], although here again I differ from the public. It must be admitted that in "starts" Four "rows with his arms"; but this defect is not visible in steady rows, and the tearing at stroke of Four and Bow [David Campbell-Muir] are occasional rather than permanent faults. Four appears also to "rush his slide"; but here again it must be remembered that he has a longer body to dispose of than other members of the crew, that he sits high and has long arms, and that it is impossible for him with such conformation to slide in exactly the same way as Three [Edward Taylor], with whom the eye instinctively compares him.

The writer wrote that in any case, 'we ought again to have a magnificent race'. In his article, he also mentioned that Trevor-Jones was absent, but Muttlebury was still around to help the crew, and 'he has never taken greater pain with a crew, and no crew has ever better repaid those pains by steady and progressive improvement'.

Sir Charles Dilke then counted up some disadvantages that came to be well-used reasons during the mid-1890s why Cambridge was so unlucky in their attempt to beat Oxford in the Boat Race: the finest oarsmen of Eton were rowing for Oxford, with the exception of Dudley-Ward, but it was also the case, as Sir Charles put it, that 'one swallow does not make a summer' (he seemed to have forgotten that president Bell also had rowed at Eton); the 'imperfection' of the River Cam; and some harm had to be accredited to the fact of the huge size of Trinity College, and wrote Sir Charles, 'the unmanageable character of the First Trinity Boat Club, which, while having the greatest choice of powerfully built public-school men of any club, seldom contributes members to the university eight, and is never head of the river at Cambridge'.

Needless to say, not all oarsmen and coaches at Cambridge agreed with Sir Charles, especially not those from First Trinity BC, who were a proud group.

In an earlier era, Rudie Lehmann had dedicated a poem in honour of his club at Cambridge. His "A Trinity Boating Song" begins,

All hail! ye men from Trinity, who sport the old dark blue,
Who man the brittle cedar ship and sweep your oarblades through;
Who mark it well and far behind, and make the finish ring,
And shoot your hands like lightning out, and slowly, slowly swing;

On the day before the Boat Race, Friday 2 April 1897, the two spare-men of the crews, Gerald Bullard, Cambridge, and Robert Pitman, Oxford, sculled a race from Putney to Hammersmith – a match that Bullard won easily.

In the morning the next day, a chilly wind remained from the previous evening's cold weather. Rain clouds moved in, which led to a cold, light drizzle before the race, set to start at 2:15 p.m. In the middle of the day, huge crowds of people moved around the banks of the Thames to head for Putney, Hammersmith, Chiswick, Barnes, Mortlake and other favourite spectator spots along the course. More than the usual number of steamers, tugs, barges and rowboats were moving upstream on the river. Only four steamers were going to be allowed to follow the two eights when the contest was on: one from each university, one for the umpire (which also took the coaches and other 'Old Blues') and one steamer for the gentlemen of the press, according to *The Times*.

Cambridge won the toss and chose the Middlesex station, so the Cambridge steamer and the umpire's steamer ended up on that station, while the Oxford steamer and the press steamer were closer to the Dark Blues on the Surrey side. With their choice of Middlesex, Cambridge hoped for an early lead, giving them the inside of the first bend at Craven Steps.

As the challenger, Cambridge embarked first, a little late at 2:15 p.m., closely followed by Oxford. Cambridge paddled down to Putney Bridge along the Surrey shore and made a wide row across the

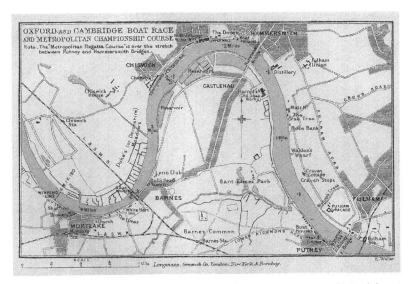

The Oxford and Cambridge Boat Race course between Putney and Mortlake, in the book *Rowing* (1898).

river before they came up on the Middlesex stake boat. Oxford, who rowed in a new eight built by John H. Clasper (Harry Clasper's son), paddled mid-river to their stake boat, which was anchored to the Surrey side. Each of the stake boats had a waterman waiting for the eights to dock their sterns.

Umpire Colonel Willan (four-time winning Oxford Blue in 1866-1869 and the same man who had made a mess of Leander and Cornell's start in the Grand at Henley two years earlier) gave both crews a couple of words of warning before he raised his pistol, with which he sent off the two boats.

The Dark Blues came to the race as favourites. Two weeks earlier the bookmakers had the odds of 3 to 1 on Oxford, but on race day it had changed to 5 to 1 on Oxford, which was a given bet. Earlier during practice, the Oxford crew had set a new course record at 18 minutes 27 seconds. Still, Cambridge had high hopes of giving Oxford a good match, as the oarsmen in the Light Blue crew were not all fresh and without skill: bow David Campbell-Muir (his first race), 2 Adam Bell (his third race), 3 Edward Taylor (his first race), 4 Hunting Howell (his first race), 5 William Bieber (his second race), 6 Drury

The Light Blue crew that raced against the Dark Blues on 3 April 1897. Back row, left to right: B. H. Howell (4, Trinity Hall), E. J. D. Taylor (3, Caius; dark jacket), W. J. Fernie (stroke, Trinity Hall; sitting) and D. E. Campbell-Muir (bow, Trinity Hall). Front row, left to right: W. A. Bieber (5, Trinity Hall), A. S. Bell (2, Trinity Hall), E. C. Hawkins (cox, Caius), W. Dudley-Ward (7, Third Trinity) and D. Pennington (6, Caius).

Pennington (his second race), 7 William Dudley-Ward (his first race), stroke William Fernie (his second race) and cox Caesar Hawkins (his first race).

With Howell making the Light Blue boat, he was the second American to row for Cambridge in the Boat Race. Rudie Lehmann's friend, Francis Peabody of Harvard, had been the first American, in 1873, when Cambridge had won by three lengths.

Gordon Ross writes in *The Boat Race: The Story of the First Hundred Races Between Oxford and Cambridge* (1954):

Cambridge made a determined bid to strive for victory in 1897, but they were really up against it. The Oxford crew is described unconditionally as the finest crew that ever rowed. It consisted of [John] de Knoop at Bow (his second race), [Geoffrey] Edwards at Two (the only new boy), [Charles] Philips at Three (his third race), [Charles] Burnell at Four (his third race),

'The finest crew that ever rowed' – the 1897 Dark Blue crew. Standing, back row, left to right: J. J. J. de Knoop (New College), R. Carr (Magdalen), H. G. Gold (stroke, Magdalen), G. O. C. Edwards (New College), D. H. McLean (coach), sitting, left to right: C. D. Burnell (Magdalen), C. K. Philips (New College), W. E. Crum (New College), E. R. Balfour (University College), in the very front, H. R. K. Pechell (cox, Brasenose).

[Ernest] Balfour at Five (his second race), [Russell] Carr at Six (his second race), [Walter] Erskine-Crum at Seven (his fourth race), [Harcourt] Gold at stroke (his second race) and [Horace] Pechell the cox (his second race); a boat-load of experience.

With the wind coming in from east-south-east and with a good running tide, the rowing conditions were going to be fast. After the start, the Light Blues took a slight lead rowing 20 strokes in the first half of the first minute, then going up to 37 strokes for the second half of the first minute – to be compared to the Dark Blues' 18 and 36. However, Oxford soon increased their stroke rate, so by the Mile Post, they were one second in front of Cambridge. At the Crab Tree, Oxford had slightly more than a canvas lead and now they began to push harder.

Passing under Hammersmith Bridge, Cambridge was almost a full boat length down, and with Oxford rowing beautifully well together, it would be hard for Cambridge to catch up. The Dark Blues were still ahead at Chiswick Reach and Eyot, and passing Chiswick Steps, they had a nine-second lead. It did not help that Cambridge put in a spurt now and then; Oxford had a comfortable lead, which at Chiswick Church had become four lengths. Thereafter both crews came into rough water due to a strong wind, and Cambridge did not manage to close in on their opponents. According to an article in *The Times*, at this stage Oxford were 'not doing more than a strong paddle' with 31 strokes per minute, while Cambridge did nearly 35.

At one point the Light Blues felt the wash from the Dark Blue's bow side oars, so Hawkins steered his boat over to be directly behind Oxford's boat, some three lengths down. 'It was a case of follow my leader thence to Barnes Bridge, reached by the Oxonians in 16 min. exactly, Cambridge being 11 sec. in the rear', *The Times* wrote. Coming out of Barnes Bridge, the crews were met with a fair wind that followed them to the finish. Oxford kept a steady stroke at 32 and crossed the finish line at 19 minutes 11.4 seconds, two and a third boat lengths ahead of Cambridge who put in a spurt at the end, passing the finishing post with a rate of 38 strokes per minute.

Howell and his fellow Cambridge oarsmen had made a brave effort to overtake the Dark Blues, who won their eighth consecutive race. However, Cambridge had not just competed against a good Oxford crew, they had raced and lost to 'the finest crew that ever rowed'.

After the Cambridge loss in the Boat Race, coach Trevor-Jones found it necessary to publicly explain why the Light Blues had lost again. He did this in a signed article published in *The Cambridge Review* in April 1897. In his piece, Trevor-Jones echoed what Sir Charles Dilke had written in his article in *The Saturday Review*. Among Cambridge's 'disadvantages' and problems were, Trevor-Jones counted up, a) that Eton oarsmen went to Oxford, not Cambridge, b) 'it is impossible to maintain a light and lively style on the thick and shallow waters' of the Cam, c) he felt personally ridiculed by anonymous writers in magazines and papers like *Truth*, *Isis* and others, d) Cambridge got no help from Old Blues, with the exception of Muttlebury, e) and, here he was really asking for trouble, the 'present cramped and stilted style' of First Trinity men is such, that 'when they get into mixed crews, they fail utterly to assimilate with the members of those crews'.

A response from William B. Close of First Trinity was rapidly published in *The Cambridge Review* on 29 April. Close had rowed in three Boat Races: a losing crew in 1875, a winning in 1876 and the dead heat race in 1877. Although Close in the beginning of his letter called Trevor-Jones 'my friend', he then used two and a half pages in *The Cambridge Review* – these were the days when a magazine editor did not shorten a letter writer's ranting – to strongly oppose Trevor-Jones's views, using the most explicit language. Close only partially agreed with one of Trevor-Jones's five reasons for Oxford having been more successful than Cambridge during the 1890s and that is 'the ready-made Eton oars [are] going to Oxford'. However, the First Trinity man thought that Cambridge should 'make their own oars and not look for ready-made oars'.

To the Cambridge coach's second reason, that it was 'impossible' to really get good practise on the Cam, Close replied: 'I will admit that under Mr. Trevor-Jones' tuition it does appear impossible', but many good crews have been rowing on the Cam, and 'I have no patience with those who blame our old Cam for the faults of style in Cambridge rowing'. Furthermore, Close thought that it was 'humiliating' to Cambridge University BC that one of their coaches confessed to being 'hampered' by anonymous Oxford correspondents. Close wrote, 'In my time, twenty years ago, we had the same thing to put up with from anonymous writers, and Mr. [Walter 'Guts'] Woodgate and others were just as offensive to the C.U.B.C. in the press as they have been of late years; but we did not pay the slightest attention to him or to them, and Sir, we used to win races against Oxford'.

To answer the fourth reason, Close wrote that 'Mr. Muttlebury is perhaps the only old Blue outside Trinity Hall sufficiently good-natured to attempt to finish a crew rowing after the fashion inculcated by Mr. Trevor-Jones'.

There had been other 'old oars', like Close's older brother James B., who was elected Cambridge University BC president in 1894, the year before he was mentioned by Owen Seaman in his poem "Of those that go down to the River". Furthermore, James B. Close was also the coach of First Trinity BC during this time, the mid-1890s. But the fact was, William B. Close stated, that no old Blues had been seriously approached since Trevor-Jones took over the coaching at the Hall. Close also revealed that in 1895 it had been suggested that Cambridge University BC should ask Oxford coach Ducker McLean to come over to Cambridge 'to bring back the lost style'. But, wrote Close, neither Theodore Hope (1896 president) nor Adam Bell (1897 president), both Hall men, had approached McLean with the question.

If William Close had tried to fairly understand Trevor-Jones's four first reasons, he was in total disagreement with the last and fifth reason, where the Hall coach mentioned that the oarsmen of First Trinity were impossible to mix with other oarsmen because of their 'cramped and stilted style'. Trevor-Jones had also written that the First Trinity oarsmen were 'non-existent as material for the authorities to draw on' in a Blue boat. Close used one-and-a-half magazine pages for his heavy bombardment to try to totally pulverise Trevor-Jones's last theory. There was no mistake of Close's deep indignation when he wrote: 'This, Sir, is from the pen of him who is responsible for the attempt lately made to assimilate the different styles of Dudley Ward and Bell, Pennington and Bieber, Fernie and Howell!' Close went on to say:

… who can doubt that when Mr. Trevor-Jones talks of the rest of the university he means Trinity Hall; and thus we have a distinct treat from the recognised Coach in Trinity Hall, that unless (which the heavens forbid) First and Third Trinity, Caius, Lady Margaret, and any other college row in the fashion now in vogue at Trinity Hall, they shall not row in the university crew if Mr. Trevor-Jones can help it but shall be boycotted. After this deluge – and I hope Mr. Trevor-Jones may find those waters lively enough!

For several years during the 1890s, Close wrote, many good oarsmen from First and Third Trinity had been overlooked while second-rated oarsmen from Trinity Hall have been selected by a Hall president to row in the Blue boat. As an example, he mentioned that there were 'two weak Hall men […] this year, […who] completely extinguished any chance Cambridge had of developing into a really fast crew, though there are several stronger and better oarsmen at

THE CAMBRIDGE CREW OF 1898.

["Sandow, the strong man, has offered to train the Cambridge crew on his own system, and undertakes to turn out such a crew as has not been seen for years."—*Daily Paper*.]

Owing to their magnificent development and the consequent crowding of the Boat, but little headway could be made during the Race, and at the moment when Oxford was passing the Winning-post, the above Crew was laboriously endeavouring to "negotiate" Hammersmith Bridge! (Our Artist's Apologies are due to "Bow," who, owing to the exigencies of space, is but partially portrayed. It is only fair to him to say that in beauty and physique he is in no way inferior to the rest of the Crew !)

On 25 September 1897 the magazine *Punch* interpreted some news from the *Daily Paper*, which wrote: 'Sandow, the strong man, has offered to train the Cambridge crew on his own system, and undertakes to turn out such a crew as has not been seen for years.'

Punch wrote: 'Owing to their magnificent development and the consequent crowding of the boat, but little headway could be made during the Race, and at the moment when Oxford was passing the winning-post, the above crew was laboriously endeavouring to "negotiate" Hammersmith Bridge! (Our artist's apologies are due to "bow", who owing to the exigencies of space, is but partially portrayed. It is only fair to him to say that in beauty and physique he is in no way inferior to the rest of the crew!).'

Eugen Sandow (1867-1925) was the stage name of Friedrich Wilhelm Müller, a German circus athlete and pioneering strong man, known as the 'father of modern bodybuilding'.

Cambridge'. Without mentioning any names it was quite obvious that the 'weak Hall men' were Howell and Campbell-Muir. 'We must conclude' Close wrote, 'that Trevor-Jones, as a resident Coach, hypnotises the minds of the Hall rowing authorities year by year with his unfortunate rowing notions and theories'.

In all this chaos, Close saw only one solution. There was already a saviour among the Cambridge oarsmen, at least the way Close pictured it. The man to save rowing at Cambridge was the freshman, William Dudley-Ward of Third Trinity, the ex-Captain of the Boats at

Eton: 'I sincerely hope that he will be the next President of C.U.B.C.', Close wrote. This head-to-head collision between Trinity Hall and First Trinity quickly became news. *Country Life Illustrated* wrote in an article on 8 May that whether Trevor-Jones was right or wrong, Cambridge was in need of a uniformed rowing style throughout all the boat clubs. The paper also stated:

Oxford has accomplished this difficult task, thanks in a great measure to what may be called the system of universal coaching [...] Not a little of Oxford's success is due to Mr. Fletcher's insistence on this principle. There is scarcely a boat on the Isis that has not learnt the elements of the Eton style from Mr. Fletcher himself, and most of the other coaches have followed him in putting aside to some extent the interests of their separate colleges.

It would undoubtedly have surprised the writer of the article if he knew that a year later William Fletcher would actually coach Cambridge's Blue boat.

The 1897 Trinity Hall Double Sculls: Hunting Howell and Gerald Bullard.

The Trinity Hall crew that won the 1897 Head of the River. Standing, back row, left to right: Unidentified (probably the spareman), coach Henry Trevor-Jones, Lancelot Baines, Hunting Howell and Gerald Bullard. Sitting, left to right: David Campbell-Muir, William Bieber, William Fernie (captain and stroke), Adam Bell and Noel Calvert. Sitting, in front: Francis Foster (cox).

The next races for Trinity Hall BC after the Boat Race were during May term. The boat club had high expectations as five members of the Hall had rowed in the Light Blue crew and to those oarsmen could be added Gerald Bullard and Charles Steele who had earned their Trial caps the previous December. The Trinity Hall oarsmen met with success: the combination William Fernie (Trinity Hall) and William Dudley-Ward (Third Trinity) won the Magdalene Pairs, Gerald Bullard and Hunting Howell took the Lowe Double Sculls and Trinity Hall's first eight kept the Headship with ease. In the Trinity Hall's winning first eight rowed, from the bow, David Campbell-Muir, Noel Calvert, Gerald Bullard, Hunting Howell, Lancelot Baines, Adam Bell, William Bieber, stroke William Fernie and cox Francis Foster. Fernie was captain of the club and Trevor-Jones was, of course, the coach.

The 1897 Henley Royal Regatta: on the right, the finish line and the Judge's Box. In the middle of the photo is the boathouse where Howell stayed during the regatta – notice the American flag on its roof.

At Henley Royal Regatta between 14 and 16 July 1897, Trinity Hall won its first heat in the Grand by beating the London RC. However, the Hall crew lost to New College precisely as they had done the previous year. New College went on to take the cup by overcoming a Leander crew. Bell and Fernie advanced to the final in the Silver Goblets, but lost to Ernest Balfour and Guy Nickalls of Leander. The Trinity Hall pair led by a length and a half at Fawley, but there Bell was seized with a cramp, whereupon he and Fernie gave up the race.

With the Hall's first eight out of the game in the Grand, Howell could concentrate on another cup, the Diamond Challenge Sculls. He had sculled since last October, but would nine months of practice in a single scull – minus weeks of absence in the boat due to a frozen Cam, illness and practice with the Light Blue crew – be enough to compete against the best scullers in England, if not in the world?

Howell had a lucky draw and had his first heat in the second round where he met G. McHenry of Thames RC. McHenry had sculled in the Diamonds before, in 1892 for a Paris club and in 1893 in the colours of Thames RC. Hunting did not have any problems winning his first race in the Diamonds.

In his next heat, he raced against his countryman from Wachusett BC, Massachusetts, Edward 'Ned' Hanlan Ten Eyck, named after the Canadian world professional sculling champion, who was his godfather. Ten Eyck, who was four years Howell's junior, had been allowed to enter the Diamonds despite the fact that the Henley

Artist Henry Charles Seppings Wright gave this view from the Grosvenor Club Enclosure (later to be The Remenham Club) of the final heat of the 1897 Diamonds between Harry Blackstaffe (on the Bucks side) and Ned Hanlan Ten Eyck (on the Berks side) in *The Illustrated London News* on 24 July 1897. St. Mary's Church is a well-recognised landmark in the background. Like many other images on rowing and boat racing, this features the spectators and the liveliness on the riverbank, while the race is a secondary event in the background.

Stewards suspected him of being a professional. This assumption was mainly based on his coach, his father James Ten Eyck, who was a well-known professional oarsman. Needless to say, it did not help that the 17-year-old sculler, small in stature at his 5ft. 8 in. (173 cm), was an American; the 1895 scandal involving Cornell and its professional coach was still fresh in everyone's memory.

There was actually another American sculler in the Diamonds this year, W. S. McDowell of Delaware BC, who easily defeated the two previous years' winner, Rupert Guinness, who sculled for Thames RC.

The irritation that was to be found among certain men in the English rowing establishment about the American oarsmen seemed not to affect or relate to Hunting Howell. In his case it was different, as he was racing in the black and white colours of a well-respected Cambridge college. Furthermore, he had taken up the oar first when he began studying at Trinity Hall. Howell was thereby molded in the proper English way and from him no 'dirty tricks' were to be expected.

The Trinity Hall man rowed a great race, but in the end, Ten Eyck beat him, but only by a quarter of a length. In the final, in a new record time, 8 minutes 35 seconds, Ten Eyck easily defeated Harry Blackstaffe of Vesta RC who sculled in his first final of the Diamonds. Even Blackstaffe, whose friends called him 'Blackie', had in the beginning of his rowing career had difficulty being regarded as an amateur, as he was working in the meat trade. Before the winning ceremony, some of Blackie's friends urged him to protest the result as Ten Eyck, in their eyes, was a professional. However, Blackstaffe refused, as he saw a protest as an unsportsmanlike gesture.

To celebrate his victory, poor Ten Eyck did everything wrong, at least in the eyes of the English rowing press. He and his father 'attended a dinner given in honour of himself and his father at the Half Moon at Putney by all the best known English professionals' Geoffrey Page writes in his superb *Hear the Boat Sing: The History of Thames Rowing Club and Tideway Rowing* (1991), and continues 'This surely was an open confession of guilt'.

In the 1898 issue of the *Rowing Almanack and Oarsman's Companion*, its editor Edwin D. Brickwood, signature 'Argonaut' (Diamonds winner in 1859 and 1862 and champion of the Wingfields in 1861), reflected on the passed rowing season, when he wrote about Ned Ten Eyck: 'the very strong presumption from his parentage, his associations, and his appearance, that he was by no means of the British type of amateur, still less a gentleman amateur'. In his article Brickwood mentioned all the professionals who were present at Ten Eyck's celebration banquet at the Half Moon, the boat builders John H. Clasper, George Sims and W. Winship, and the famous oarsmen Tom Sullivan, Bill Barry, Charles 'Wag' Harding, Bill East and twenty others. Brickwood sourly rounded it up with a Latin phrase: *Noscilu e sociis* – 'It is known from its associates'.

For the 1898 Henley Royal Regatta, the Stewards turned down Ten Eyck's application to defend his title in the Diamonds.

In spite of his loss to Ten Eyck in the 1897 Diamonds, Howell had proved that he was a man to count on in the single sculls. He had talent, obviously, and was working hard, but to reach the ultimate success as a sculler he needed a good trainer. It was after the 1897 season was over that one of the best English sculling coaches began giving Howell tutorials, the well-liked professional English ex-champion, William 'Bill' G. East.

Bill East was born in 1866 in London and legend has it that he always stayed close to the Thames. At sixteen years of age, he became an apprentice to a waterman. Coming out of his apprenticeship in 1887, East won the Doggett's Coat and Badge Race. Four years later, in November 1891, he beat G. J. Pearkins on the 'north river', the Tyne in Newcastle, for the English professional sculling championship. East never defended his title, which went to George Bubear, who defeated George Hosmer of Boston, USA, in a race for the title on the River Thames in January 1893.

Rowing historian Neil Wigglesworth writes about the professionals: 'The professionalization of rowing had the effect of producing a racing elite amongst the watermen of England which in turn produced personalities whose popularity often remained after their racing careers were over. This enabled many to secure employment in coaching and training amateur club oarsmen'.

WM G·EAST·
ENGLISH OARSMAN.

William 'Bill' G. East, Doggett's Coat and Badge winner in 1887 and English professional sculling champion in 1891, became Hunting Howell's sculling coach in 1897. East was depicted in the American tobacco company Allen & Ginter's second sports cards series (N29) in 1888.

Allen & Ginter's first sports cards came out in 1887. These cards, which were a series called N28, included 50 sports champions. Rowing historian Bill Miller writes: 'Baseball was growing rapidly at this time while the rowing professionals were losing their popularity. Still, of the 50 World Champions, oarsmen numbered ten, baseball - ten, and also pugilists - ten, wrestlers - seven, billiards players - seven, rifle shooters - four and pool players - two round out the set. Perhaps this gives us a little insight into the popularity of the various sports in the public eye at that time'. The following ten professional oarsmen were depicted in the N28 series: William Beach, John Teemer, Edward Trickett, Edward Hanlan, Wallace Ross, Jacob Gaudaur, George Hosmer, Albert Hamm, John McKay and George Bubear.

Hunting Howell with his sculling coach, Bill East, who would become Queen Victoria's waterman in 1898 and Bargemaster to King Edward VII in 1901.

The professionals came early on to be involved with rowing at Oxford and Cambridge, where they were used as coxes and coaches. However, rowing at the universities was a sport for amateur gentlemen and there was an imminent risk that a professional coxswain would try one of his tricks to win a race by, for example, fouling the opponent's boat, which was not uncommon during professional races. Oxford was the first of the two universities to give up the professionals. Cambridge, however, Eric Halladay mentions in his *Rowing in England: A Social History – The Amateur Debate* (1990), 'were more reluctant to abandon the use of watermen in training crews on the Cam'. But it happened in 1873.

Bill East never coached any Cambridge University crews, although he did act as their waterman and pilot, taking the Light Blue coxes in a boat for many years to show them how to steer on the sometimes rough waters of the Thames, with its tricky tides and streams between Putney and Mortlake. During the 1890s, East became a popular coach for amateur scullers who could pay his fees. Vivian Nickalls, Guy's younger brother, had hired East for his entry in the Diamonds in 1894.

Vivian Nickalls won the Wingfields in 1892, 1894 and 1895 and several cups at Henley, including the 1891 Diamonds. Only three scullers showed up for the Diamonds that year. In the first round Vivian easily beat G. Elin (Third Trinity BC). His brother Guy drew a bye in the first round, so the final was going to be between the Nickalls brothers. Guy 'retired' from the final, so his brother could get the title by a row-over.

The Hon. Rupert Guinness, who trained at Thames RC, but for some years raced in the colours of Leander Club at Henley, was another renowned sculler who was coached by East. Guinness sculled in the Diamonds for the first time in 1894 and was there defeated by Vivian Nickalls, who lost the final to his brother, Guy. (After the race, Guy wept 'like a child for half an hour' for having beaten his

The Hon. Rupert Guinness, who won the Diamonds in 1895 and 1896, and the Wingfields in 1896.

Guy Nickalls rowed in the Boat Race five times, winning two of the races for Oxford in 1890 and 1891. He won the Wingfields in 1887-1890 and 1894 and is one of the most successful oarsmen in the history of Henley Royal Regatta. Among his many winning cups at Henley were five victories in the Diamonds, in 1888-1890, 1893 and 1894.

younger brother.) In the next year's final of the Diamonds, Guinness easily beat Guy Nickalls, who struggled from start to finish because he had hitherto at the regatta won the Silver Goblets (with Vivian), the Stewards' and the Wyfolds.

Walter 'Guts' Woodgate, Oxford Blue, a winner of the Wingfields, Diamonds and other cups at Henley, and a writer and critic on rowing matters, wrote a race report in *Vanity Fair*: 'It was temporary insanity of Guy Nickalls, glutton for work and stayer though he is, to tackle a vastly improved sculler like young Guinness in the final "Diamonds" heat after the severe prior races and on the leeward station, while Guinness was fresh'. Although Woodgate's empathy was with his friend Guy Nickalls, he recognised that Guinness was an up-and-coming man as he wrote that Guinness 'will become a clinker' – a first-rate sculler.

Later in July 1895, in the runner-up race for the Wingfield Sculls, the amateur championships of the Thames and Great Britain, with Vivian Nickalls being the holder of the title, Guy pulled a muscle in his arm when he was ahead of Guinness, who then passed him. However, with twenty yards left, Nickalls found himself level with Guinness. He tried a spurt, but suddenly one of his swivels opened up and he capsized. 'We both literally floated together over the winning post, but, as he was in his boat and I was not, he naturally won', Guy

Walter Bradford 'Guts' Woodgate rowed in two winning Oxford crews in the Boat Race, 1862 and 1863. He won the Wingfields in 1862, 1864 and 1867, and between 1861 and 1868 he took eight titles at Henley, including the Diamonds in 1864. After his rowing career had come to an end, 'Guts' became a feared rowing critic with a sharp eye for details.

Nickalls wrote in his *Life's a Pudding*, his autobiography which was posthumously edited and published in 1939 by his son, G. O. 'Gully' Nickalls.

In the final, Vivian Nickalls beat Guinness and won the championship. The next year, 1896, Guinness got his revenge when he defeated Vivian Nickalls in the Wingfields. Earlier that summer, Guinness had also won the Diamonds and the London Cup, the Senior Sculls at the Metropolitan Regatta, which was organised by the London RC. With the addition of the Wingfields, he took what is called the 'Triple Crown'. Having Bill East as a coach seemed to pay off well in medals and cups.

Guts Woodgate also wrote a report in *Vanity Fair* about the final race in the 1896 Diamonds – words that could well describe the situation Hunting Howell would find himself in a year later, having to *row* first in the Light Blue eight and then in the Hall's first eight during May term, followed by the Grand, and then after that *scull* in the Diamonds. Woodgate wrote about the problems that Vivian Nickalls faced for the 1896 Diamonds:

The sculling was of a higher class than I can remember. I have seen better scullers than Guinness, the winner – e.g., Guy Nickalls – when at his best, the late T.C. Edwardes-Moss and (young) Frank Playford; but I never saw so many rivals each of whom was better than many a man whose name stands on the silver plates of the Diamonds box – V. Nickalls, Swann, and Beaumont as instances. To have been the best in such a field is of itself a record in the annals of the prize. V. Nickalls was handicapped by handling an oar in two other crews, while his opponents could stick solely to sculling. My estimate of the detraction of oars upon sculling practice is this: If A and B are dead-level scullers on the 1st of April, then A goes to work with an oar, and grinds regularly and hard in a crew (in order to keep that crew going, and to get it into condition), and only sculls in spare moments up to the 1st of July, while B meantime devotes himself solely to sculling, B will be some four lengths better in a nine minutes' race than A by the 1st of July; and it will take A another two or three months exclusive sculling after that to get back to level terms with B.

The reason is that the main speed in sculling depends on level actions of hands – into the water and out of it. If one hand gets one-twentieth of a second start or a fraction of an inch more stretch, or one blade varies one degree of an angle in the water, the boat turns to the pressure: then the advantage stolen by the one hand has to be abandoned and eased off before the end of the same stroke, in order to bring the keel straight. All this is waste of power and loss of speed. Now, an oar does not work a man all through in one plane; hence it tends to produce some irregularity in sculling action when the oarsman presently uses the same muscles from a sculling seat. Still more, the time spent at the oar is lost to sculling practice.

For the 1897 Wingfield Sculls, Rupert Guinness did not defend his title, though he raced in the Diamonds two week before, now in the colours of Thames RC, and was defeated in his first heat by the American W. S. McDowell.

With Guinness not racing, there were five competitors for the Wingfield Sculls in July: R. K. Beaumont (Thames RC); F. Beddington (Medway RC); Harry Blackstaffe (Vesta RC), who two days earlier had taken the London Cup; A. F. G. Everitt (London RC); and Hunting Howell (Trinity Hall).

Under normal circumstances Howell, as a non-Brit, would not be allowed to scull for the amateur championship. However, the Wingfields organisation committee did permit Howell to take part in the race. Regrettably, the minutes from the Wingfields committee meetings for the 1897 race were lost a long time ago, so it is impossible to really know the reasons behind the committee's decision. A good guess in this case would be that Howell was seen more as a Cambridge sculler than an unpredictable American oarsman.

On the day of the Wingfields race, on 21 July, some light rain had passed during the morning, but in time for the race the weather was fine with a slight breeze from the west. At the start, Everitt took a quick lead, but at Craven Steps, Beddington and Blackstaffe were level with him. Soon Blackstaffe broke loose and approaching Hammersmith Bridge the Vesta sculler was four lengths ahead of Everitt, who was two lengths in front of Beaumont, who had Howell a half length down. At the Doves, Hunting passed Beaumont, and at Chriswick Eyot, when Everitt started to have problems with his steering, Howell caught up and passed him at Chiswick Ferry. Blackstaffe reached Barnes Bridge in 20 minutes 12 seconds, eight lengths in front of Howell, who was six lengths ahead of Everitt. Blackstaffe crossed the finish line above the Ship Inn at Mortlake in 23 minutes 58 seconds, with a four lengths lead over Howell, who was six lengths ahead of Everitt. Both Beddington and Beaumont had rowed out and did not finish. *The Times* reported the day after the race, that 'All three had sculled well, especially the winner, who was unfortunate in being obliged to meet E. H. Ten Eyck at Henley Regatta in the final heat of the Diamond Challenge Sculls'.

During Michaelmas term, Hunting Howell was involved in a nasty accident while practicing for the Colquhoun Sculls, a short note read in *The Times* on 14 October 1897. While sculling at full speed on the Cam, Hunting collided with another sculler, who also went at full speed. The bow of the other shell pierced Howell's boat and went right through the calf of his right leg just below his knee. The other sculler could not back away as there was a risk in extracting the bow from Howell's calf as it would probably cause a major blood loss. A man at shore swam out with a saw, so Howell could saw off the bow, while it was still penetrating his leg. Then Howell was towed to shore and carried into a boathouse where a surgeon removed the piece of wood and took care of the wound.

Howell was confined to his bed for a few weeks, but was out practicing on the river again in December – in a boat with a fixed seat so he did not need to bend his legs. In an article published in *Harper's Weekly* two years later, in August 1899, telling a reporter about the

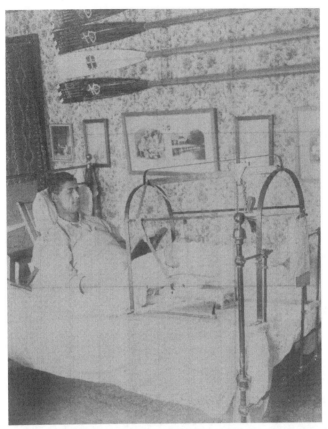

Hunting Howell tied to his bed after he had collided with another sculler on the Cam in October 1897. In December, he was back out on the river. Notice the trophy blades hanging on the wall, some of them from winning the 'Head' in the May Races.

accident, Howell said that he regarded the piece of wood as one of his 'rowing trophies'.

With Howell out of the picture, Trinity Hall BC had to rearrange their crew in the Light Four as well. The rapidly put-together new four was very successful that Michaelmas term, winning all the races. The members of the crew were, bow Bevan Charles Cox, 2 Adam

The successful 1897 Trinity Hall BC's Light Four: stroke Charles Steele, 3 Gerald Bullard, 2 Adam Bell and bow Charles Cox.

Bell, 3 Gerald Bullard and stroke Charles Steele. (After his studies, in 1901, Cox tried farming in New Brunswick before he came back to England to be the editor of the rowing column of *The Field* between 1903 and 1920. He then wrote under the signature 'Old Blue' in the *Daily Telegraph* between 1921 and 1927.)

At the Trial eights in December 1897, the Hall's Gerald Bullard, Noel Calvert and Henry Wright (cox) were in the winning crew, and Charles Hole and Charles Steele (stroke) in the losing crew.

With his fresh leg wound, Hunting Howell did not go for the Trial eights. As an Old Blue, and if his leg healed and he stayed healthy in general, he for certain would have a seat in the Light Blue boat in the race on 26 March 1898, especially as he had improved since the last Boat Race.

Howell went home to New York for Christmas, arriving on 18 December via the steamship RMS *Lucania* from Liverpool. With him were his fellow oarsmen from Cambridge, Claude Goldie and William Fernie. In a short article in the *New York Times* on 19 December, Fernie denied a rumour claiming that he and Goldie were on their way to New Haven to coach the Yale crew. Meeting the oarsmen in

New York was Rudie Lehmann, who had just come from Washington, D.C., where he had dined with and been celebrated by Teddy Roosevelt, now Assistant Secretary of the Navy, who was an avid rower. Lehmann was still coaching Harvard's crew and he took Goldie and Fernie to Cambridge. Howell, on the other hand, went home to Brooklyn.

After William Fernie and William Dudley-Ward had won the Magdalene Pairs during May term 1897, *Country Life Illustrated* published a little note about their victory on 5 June. The magazine also wrote that Dudley-Ward had been elected president of Cambridge University BC, which 'seems to give satisfaction both in Cambridge and outside it, holding out a hope of a reinvigorating change, of which Cambridge rowing at this time seems to be in peculiar need'.

Already in an article in mid-February the same year, the magazine had predicted that Dudley-Ward, despite the fact that he was a freshman, was going to be appointed president of Cambridge University BC, which had been the hopes of William Close when he went to battle against Henry Trevor-Jones in *The Cambridge Review* after the 1897 Boat Race.

In spite of the high hopes that emerged with Dudley-Ward's presidency, there were some rumblings of discontent in the ranks. Regardless of Dudley-Ward's record as a fine oarsman at Eton, he was still in his first year at Cambridge and some of the oarsmen at Cambridge, presumably mostly the Hall men, thought that it was Fernie who should have become president. Maybe things did not look that good for Cambridge at the end of 1897 after all.

CHAPTER 5
1898: Record Sculling Champion

To make things worse, at least in the eyes of many Cambridge oarsmen, for the 1898 Boat Race president Dudley-Ward brought in the renowned Oxford oarsman and coach William Fletcher to coach Cambridge. Fletcher had rowed for the winning Dark Blues in 1890, 1891, 1892 and 1893, and had a large number of pots from Henley. Because of this bold move Dudley-Ward 'encountered great opposition, several men refusing to row', Christopher Dodd writes in *The Oxford & Cambridge Boat Race* (1983).

In February 1898, the rift peaked in a meeting at the Goldie Boathouse between the captains of the boat clubs. Rudie Lehmann, back from the USA, had been invited to take the chair. President Dudley-Ward complained that Hunting Howell, now captain of Trinity Hall BC, and Adam Bell refused to row in the university boat. Howell was also accused of influencing other Hall oarsmen not to row. Raymond Etherington-Smith chimed in saying that he had had a conversation with Howell who wanted Fernie as president instead of Dudley-Ward. Howell denied that he had influenced any rower not to row for Cambridge.

The Times wrote in an account of the meeting that Lehmann pleaded to the oarsmen to end the quarrel and concentrate on 'the great struggle against Oxford'. The conflict created quite a stir in the English newspapers and was also picked up by *The New York Times* which, on 13 February, published a short piece with the head line: "Split in the

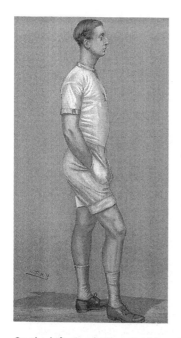

On the left, Cambridge president William Dudley-Ward depicted by 'SPY'. On the right, the Oxford coach William Fletcher, who started coaching Cambridge in 1898, also depicted by 'SPY'.

Cambridge Crew – B. H. Howell Denies Charges Brought Against Him by Dudley Ward". Two days later, on 15 February, *The Times* reported about a meeting held at Trinity Hall where a resolution was passed saying that the college had 'confidence in Mr. Howell as captain of Trinity Hall Boat Club'. A motion was also agreed upon that 'Messars. Bell and Howell be requested to place their services at the disposal of the C.U.B.C.' After this, Bell returned to his position as number two in the boat, kicking out Henry Oakeley. Howell did not, however, join the crew.

Nowadays, this is a forgotten dispute in the history of the Boat Race, but it made Howell the first American 'mutineer', who preceded the more famous rebels at Oxford in 1959 and 1987.

Indisputably, William Fletcher was a brilliant coach and did greatly improve the Cambridge crew in spite of only having three Old Blues in the boat, Dudley-Ward, Bell and Hawkins, the cox. But the crew was struck with misfortune. Getting closer to race day, the stroke Charles Steele went down with influenza and could not row. Then, the president was ordered by his doctor not to row. It was a reluctant Adam Bell, now the 'old man' in the crew, who moved from the number two seat to the stroke seat. On race day, the crew looked as follows: bow William Rennie, 2 John Beale, 3 Harold Brown, 4 Sydney Pearson, 5 Arthur Swanston, 6 Raymond Etherington-Smith, 7 Claude Goldie, stroke Adam Bell and cox Caesar Hawkins. In the Oxford boat, there were seven Old Blues, including the cox, Geoffrey Edwards, Charles Philips, Charles Burnell, Russell Carr, Auberon Herbert, Harcourt Gold and Horace Pechell. To those could be added Robert Pitman of the renowned rowing family, who had been the spareman in 1897, and Felix Warre, son of the famous coach and headmaster of Eton.

The weather on 26 March 1898 was ghastly. The tide was strong and a blizzard swept over London. Icy rain came down on the Thames and a 'crop of white horses' were seen on the Surrey side. Oxford won the toss and picked the Middlesex station, which left the Light Blues in the unruly water on the Surrey side. After half a dozen strokes at the start, the Cambridge boat was filled with water. They moved over to the shelter on the Middlesex side, but by the time they were behind Oxford, their boat was waterlogged. For the rest of the race, the Cambridge oarsmen were sliding back and forth in the icy water in the boat. The cox Hawkins sat still in the cold water and with a bitter wind and needle rain stinging his face.

How the artist Walter James illustrated a Boat Race cox in R. P. P. Rowe and C. M. Pitman's book *Rowing* (1898).

Oxford won the race in 22 minutes 15 seconds with Cambridge only 44 seconds behind. 'The remarkable thing', Henry Bond wrote, 'being that Cambridge rowed in good form from beginning to end, never going to pieces or getting ragged'. This was the Dark Blues' ninth consecutive victory.

On 12 May 1898, Bell and Howell rowed a dead heat against Goldie and Etherington-Smith for the Magdalene Pairs and five days later both crews met again, now for the Lowe Double Sculls. This time Goldie and Etherington-Smith won, at 7 minutes 27 seconds, breaking the old record by seven seconds. At the Head of the River, the Hall – with Howell in the six seat – which had held the Headship since 1890, and with only one loss since 1886, was bumped by First Trinity. Bond wrote: 'Even a Trinity Hall man may admit that an occasional change in the Headship is a good thing for the rowing of the University generally, much as he may have disliked the downfall when it came'.

In May 1898, the Cambridge University BC Pairs (Magdalene Pairs) resulted in a dead-heat between Hunting Howell and Adam Bell against Claude Goldie and Raymond Etherington-Smith. Bell, who had rowed at Eton, was a remarkable oar. He won every open event on the Cam.

Certainly, Howell was unhappy with the loss of the Headship, but other, more cheerful things were probably on his mind during this term: he was soon to take his degree. It also meant that his social calendar was filled. There were tea parties, balls and other social gatherings to attend and at some of them a photographer was there to immortalize Howell and his fellow graduates. Some of these photographs are to be found in the photo album that once belonged to Howell and which now is in the care of the National Rowing Foundation (NRF) in the USA. Among the people in some of the photographs is also a beautiful young lady, Hunting Howell's sister, Erla Louise Howell.

With all the time Howell put into training and racing during his time at Trinity Hall, his B.A. degree was maybe not as glorious as his rowing career at the college. He had studied for the general exam and got a Third. Though, on this matter, Tim Koch writes, 'a Third was entirely appropriate [for Howell]. It was known as "A Gentleman's

May Week Tea Party in 1898. Hunting with a cute parasol on the left. The parasol probably belonged to his sister, Erla, who is sitting in the front row, second from right.

Degree" or "An Oarsman's Degree"'. Also remember, Koch writes, cousin Jasper's advice to Charles Ryder at Oxford in *Brideshead Revisited*: 'You want either a First or a Fourth. There is no value in anything in between. Time spent on a good Second is time thrown away' (of course, this was Oxford where they for a long time also had a Fourth).

At Henley Royal Regatta, which was held on 5-7 July 1898, the Hall's first eight, which had lost the Headship a few weeks earlier, did not meet with success in the Grand either. The Cambridge boat, with Howell in the six seat, Bell at seven and with Steele as stroke, lost to a good crew from the London RC by two lengths.

Howell also raced in the Diamonds. In his first heat, he sculled against A. F. G. Everitt of the London RC. The American had a comfortable lead at Fawley Court Boathouse with four lengths, which became seven, eight lengths at Ishmian Club Enclosure, finally winning easily in 8 minutes 32 seconds. His next opponent was another London man, H. W. Stout, whom Howell beat by six lengths in 8 minutes 44 seconds. By then, Howell was in the final of the Diamonds, the other finalist being Harry Blackstaffe, who had defeated him in the Wingfields the previous summer.

In the final heat, Howell, who was slow at the start, managed to take a lead by a few feet at half-distance, and then get half a length at the three-quarter mile post. Crossing the finish line, Howell was three and a half lengths ahead of Blackstaffe, winning in the new record time of 8 minutes 29 seconds, which was six seconds faster than Ten Eyck's record time from the previous year. It was the first time since the Diamonds was first sculled in 1844 that a man from Trinity Hall BC had won the cup.

In the report for the 1898 Henley Royal Regatta, the Stewards expressed concerns about the 'pleasure boats' at the regatta:

The committee have to record, with great regret, that in several races the competitors were obstructed by a mass of boats protruding on the course, and in one instance by a punt drifting, through incompetent management, on to the course. The Committee feel that protection must be afforded to competitors, and, if necessary, the course must be boomed on both sides and pleasure-boats prohibited from going on the course

Hunting Howell, sitting second from the right in the middle row, a gentleman with an 'Oarsman's Degree'.

Hunting Howell, in the middle in the back row, did not only row at Cambridge, he was also a member of different societies and clubs. Here is a photograph of the Storks Literary Club in 1898, with Adam Bell on Howell's left. Gerald Bullard is sitting on the far right. Each member of the Storks had the name of one of the Greek muses, Howell being 'Urania', the goddess of music, song and dance.

The 1898 'Crescents': Howell in the front row, second from right. On his right is Adam Bell, who on his right has Gerald Bullard. Behind Howell, on his left, is Charles Steele. The Crescent club, which was established around 1609, was compiled by Trinity Hall's most distinguished sportsmen.

Members of the 1898 'Black & Whites': Howell is in the back row, second from left. Black & White was for members of the Trinity Hall BC who had rowed four terms or more.

Trinity Hall Ball Room in June 1898.

Trinity Hall Ball Stewards 1898. Howell is sitting in second row, third from left.

After the 1898 Hall Ball.

After the 1898 Masonic Ball, a group photo was taken at Market Place in central Cambridge.

Trinity Hall's eight losing to London RC in the 1898 Grand Challenge Cup.

In his first heat of the 1898 Diamonds, Hunting Howell easily won over A. F. G. Everitt of London RC.

In his second heat of the 1898 Diamonds, Howell beat H. W. Stout of London RC by six boat lengths.

In the final of the 1898 Diamonds, Howell easily beat Harry Blackstaffe of Vesta RC, setting a new record at 8 min. 29 sec.

during the Regatta. Such action would be reluctantly taken by the Committee, as it would curtail the pleasure of the majority who manage their boats efficiently, and with due regards to the best interest of the regatta, which exists for boat-racing, and not as a mere water picnic.

On 22 July 1898, Hunting Howell won the trial heat for the Wingfield Sculls by beating C. H. R. Thorn of the London RC. Three days later, Howell, on the Middlesex station, was ready for his second try for the amateur championship of the Thames and Great Britain, again racing Blackstaffe, who was the holder and who had taken the London Cup at the Metropolitan Regatta the day before the trial heat. The Wingfields race 'produced a most extraordinary contest' *The Times* wrote in a report the day after the race, on 26 July.

Blackstaffe went out quickly at the start and got a good lead, while Howell, or as *The Times* wrote, 'the Cantab', was not used to the quick tide at Putney Bridge. At Putney Reach, Blackstaffe was two boat lengths ahead, which at the Mile Post had become three and a half lengths. Passing the Hammersmith Bridge, the Londoner's time was 8 minutes 53 seconds while Howell's was 9 minutes. At Barnes Bridge, Blackstaffe was four lengths in front. To the onlookers, in-

Getting ready for the 1898 Wingfield Sculls on the River Thames: Howell's seven-oared 'pilot boat' with a Doggett coxswain and the pilot in the bow seat. In the four seat is Howell's trainer, Bill East.

The start of the 1898 Wingfield Sculls above Putney Bridge. Blackstaffe closest to the camera, with his 'pilot boat' in between the stake boats. Howell and his 'pilot boat' are on the Middlesex station.

cluding the umpire Gilbert Kennedy of Kingston RC (winner of the 1893 Wingfields) on the paddle steamer that followed the race, it looked like the sculler from Vesta RC had the championship title in the bag.

With half a mile to go, Blackstaffe began to look a little unsteady in his boat and had a slight problem with his steering, but Howell was still three lengths down. Suddenly, the Hall man began a tremendous spurt, rapidly gaining on Blackstaffe, who could not respond and was 'quickly failing in strength'. All of a sudden, the Vesta man stopped rowing with 50 yards to go, totally exhausted. Howell passed him, got a couple of lengths' lead, and stopped rowing, too, all pumped out. Nonetheless, the speed of his boat took him over the finish line in the new record time of 22 minutes 57 seconds. This was the second time a Trinity Hall man had won the Wingfields. The first one was James Bayford, who was the first winner of the Henry Wingfield's Silver Sculls in 1830. James's brother, Augustus Fredrick Bayford, who also rowed for the Hall, was in the first Cambridge crew in the Boat Race in 1829.

The 1898 Wingfields was the last race Howell won in the black and white colours of the Hall. Thereafter he moved on to the Thames RC on the Tideway.

81

1898 Wingfields: a view from the steamer, Blackstaffe ahead and his 'pilot boat' on the right.

1898 Wingfields: getting close to Barnes Bridge, Blackstaffe was almost four boat lengths ahead of Howell.

About going under Barnes Bridge nearly 1 mile to the end of the course. In Howell's photo album, where this picture is to be found, it is scribbled below the photo, 'Sculler further distant a fool not in race'.

At the same time Hunting Howell won the Wingfields, Ned Ten Eyck won the American National Championships in the single sculls on the Schuylkill, Philadelphia, and later also the championship in the double sculls together with Charles Lewis.

The news about Howell's victories in the Diamonds and the Wingfields reached America and newspapers reported with great pride about the 'American Champion of England'. One example was *The Deseret News*, the Mormon newspaper in Salt Lake City, Utah, which on 10 September on its combined art and sport page showed a large drawing – not with a very good likeness – of Howell in his single scull.

Four days later, on 14 September 1898, a short piece in *The New York Times* informed that Harvard's English coach Rudie Lehmann the previous day had married Miss Alice Marie Davis in Worcester, Massachusetts. His best man was Claude Goldie, and among the ushers were Raymond Etherington-Smith and Frank Wethered of Marlow, who rowed for the Dark Blues in 1885, 1886 and 1887, and some Harvard oarsmen, among them J. H. Perkins, captain of the crew. Lehmann had met Miss Davis in Mr. and Mrs. Francis Peabody's home, where she tutored the Peabodys' daughters.

In an article about the 1898 Wingfield Sculls, it said it was 'a splendid race' between Hunting Howell and Harry Blackstaffe. Howell won in a new record time.

On the day of the article, the 42-year-old Englishman sailed with his 24-year-old American bride aboard *Majestic* to Liverpool, England. 'On arriving home at Bourne End, they were greeted with a triumphal arch, a banquet in the village and an address from the vicar', the American rowing historian Thomas Mendenhall wrote in a 1979 article about Rudie Lehmann. While his coaching had not rendered Harvard any victories, it had given the Crimson a well-needed boost for its rowing programme that would be obvious in the following years. As the true gentleman coach, Lehmann refused to get paid for his services at Harvard, which gratefully awarded him an honorary degree in October 1897.

After taking his B.A. at Trinity Hall, Hunting Howell stayed in England to work first as a manager at his father's company's office in London, then as a director at R. W. Blackwell & Company, which was selling electrical components, and had offices in London, Liverpool, Paris and New York. Howell wanted to continue to scull, and the club he picked was the Thames RC, which had been founded in 1860 as the City of London RC. At a meeting in February 1862, the name of the club was changed to the Thames RC. In 1866, the Thames RC had acquired a boathouse at Putney, which belonged to the boat builder William Styles of Isleworth. Manager for the boathouse was William East, Snr, Bill East's father.

The Deseret News on 10 September 1898 celebrated Hunting Howell, the 'American Champion of England', on almost half the newspaper's combined art and sport page.

The professional champion Bill East's strong connection with Cambridge and Thames RC was probably the main reason why many of Cambridge's rowers went to this club after they got a job in London. Therefore, Hunting was not alone among the Hall's oarsmen to row for Thames RC. In 1898, his friends William Fernie and William Bieber also joined the club, where the old Hall rower, Richard Croft, was already a member. Croft took the Colquhoun Sculls in 1893 and the Lowe Double Sculls in 1894 (together with Adam Bell). He also rowed in the Hall's first eight, winning the Head in 1894 (with Fernie and Bieber) and in 1895 (with Fernie, Bieber and Howell). Also David Campbell-Muir, who got his Blue at the same time as Howell, became a member of the club in 1898.

For the 1898 Silver Goblets at Henley, Fernie raced in the pair with A. 'Bogie' Bogle, who was 'a very difficult and aggressive crew member', Geoffrey Page writes in *Hear the Boat Sing*. For unknown reasons Bogie was not on speaking terms with Fernie on the day of the final, where they were going to race against Arthur Hutchinson

Thames RC's William Fernie and 'Bogie' Bogle trying to row each other round while they are in the lead in the final of the 1898 Silver Goblets, where they easily beat Arthur Hutchinson and Steve Fairbairn of Jesus College BC – a race that ended with a fist fight.

and Steve Fairbairn of Jesus College BC. On the way to the start, Bogie and Fernie tried to pull each other round, which they continued to do during the race. The Jesus pair took an early lead at a high rate that, nonetheless, was doomed to fail. The Thames pair soon was in the front and won comfortably. Page writes: 'They did not stop at the line. Legend has it that they continued to Marsh Lock, where they got out and fought it out on the bank. It is not recorded who won the fight, but the boat was left for the boatman to collect'.

CHAPTER 6
1899: On Top of the Game

For the 1899 Boat Race, William Fletcher coached the Light Blues with the help of Rudie Lehmann. Raymond Etherington-Smith was president of Cambridge University BC, William Dudley-Ward was fit again to row and Claude Goldie made his second appearance in the boat. The only Hall man in the crew was Noel Calvert. Cambridge won by three and one-quarter lengths and thereby stopped a straight ten-year victory run for Oxford. 'The result was due largely to the coaching of Mr. Fletcher of Oxford', Bond wrote in *A History of the Trinity Hall Boat Club*.

At Thames RC Hunting Howell continued to scull in the single, coached by East. Nevertheless, when Howell got the opportunity, in June 1899, to be coached for an outing by another professional sculler, George Towns of Newcastle, New South Wales, Australia, he took the chance.

In April 1897, the 28-year-old Towns, who had learned to scull on the Hunter River, had arrived in England. At the time, he was regarded as a 'coming man' and his financial backers back home in Newcastle had been eager to send him to England to be able to prove himself worthy to row for the professional world sculling championships in a year or two.

Australian oarsmen had dominated the professional sport of sculling since August 1884, when William Beach beat the Canadian

George Towns on the British tobacco company Ogden's cigarettes card, A Series, No. 99, 1901.

Ned Hanlan on the Parramatta River, but in September 1896 the world sculling championship title went back to Canada when Jacob Gaudaur, Ontario, defeated Jim Stanbury of New South Wales on the River Thames. In Australia, the hopes were set for Towns to claim the world title.

In a race for the professional sculling championship of England, on 21 September 1898, William 'Bill' Barry of Putney beat Towns on the championship course between Putney and Mortlake. Seven months later, on 1 May 1899, they met again and this time Towns beat Barry for the title. This should, if Towns and his backers played their cards right, open the doors for the Australian to challenge Gaudaur for the world title.

However, Towns's stay in England was followed by mishaps. The Australian newspaper *The Star* reported in an article published on 24 July (but dated 9 June) 1899, that Towns had been run into by an eight when he was training for his first meeting with Barry. Luckily, Towns only received minor injuries, though his boat was badly damaged. Then Towns had to pay forfeit to William Haines of Old Windsor, as the Australian was ill with influenza and could not race Haines. In another race, Towns rowed into a big lump of wood, which damaged his boat so he had to abandon the race (thereby losing money in stakes and bets).

In the beginning of June 1899, Towns could do with some extra cash. One easy way to do this for a professional was to give private lessons to amateur scullers, like Hunting Howell. The article incorrectly mentioned Howell as a member of Trinity Hall, but gave his titles correctly, 'English amateur champion and holder of the Diamond Sculls'.

Jacob Gaudaur was one of the professional scullers depicted on the American tobacco company Allen & Ginter sports cards, series N28, No. 23, in 1887.

JACOB GAUDAUR.

In the afternoon both scullers set off from the Leander boathouse at Putney, *The Star* wrote, sculling up the river against the tide, rowing side by side, with Towns closest to the Surrey shore. At Barn Elms, a coxed four came down with the tide, and before anyone understood the dire situation, the four ran into Towns. The larger craft's ironshod bow hit the Australian sculler in the back and missed his spine by a couple of inches, but broke two of his ribs. Towns fell overboard but managed, despite being half unconscious, to grab hold of an oar of the coxed four. The oarsmen managed to pull him into their boat, whereupon Howell gave them an order to row to the Thames RC's boathouse.

We can only imagine what went through the American's mind at this point, having a scar on his right leg to remind him about his own accident on the Cam in October 1897.

After Towns received first aid at Thames RC, he was taken to the professional sculler Tom Sullivan's house at Battersea to be examined by a doctor. Beyond the broken ribs, the part of the back where he was hit by the four's bow was bruised and swollen. *The Star* wrote: 'The accident caused a tremendous sensation at Putney, where, by reason of his good nature and gentlemanly behaviour, Towns has become a great favourite amongst "wet-bobs" of all classes'. The author of the article speculated how this accident might affect Towns's career in the future. He even went on to say that 'it is quite possible that his career as a first-class sculler has closed'.

Luckily, the Australian's career as a world-class sculler did not come to an end on that day in June. A year later, on 10 September 1900, he defended his English championship title on the championship course against his countryman James Wray. The next year, on 7 September 1901, Towns beat Gaudaur for the professional world championship title on Lake of the Woods in Ontario, Canada.

For the 1899 Henley Royal Regatta, on 5-7 July, the Stewards had ordered booms to be placed on each side of the race course to prevent pleasure boats and punts drifting out in front of the crews racing, which in the past had ruined the day for many good oarsmen. One of these unlucky oarsmen had been the young Guy Nickalls (then rowing for Magdalen College, Oxford), who, in 1887, the year Queen Victoria celebrated her Golden Jubilee, raced in his first Diamonds event, in the final. Amongst the spectators were the Prince and Princess of Wales with a Royal party on board a boat, which got surrounded by small boats and punts. These vessels soon took over half the course, so the unfortunate Nickalls, racing on the Berks side, rowed right into the Royal enthusiasts and crashed his shell. He was not offered a restart by the Henley Stewards, but he did receive a sympathetic note from the Princess of Wales through her lady-in-waiting, Mrs. W. H. Smith, hoping that he was not hurt.

Sandow's Magazine of Physical Culture reported that houseboat owners produced 'a chorus of groans and complaints' as they saw the new booms 'as a bar to the success of the meeting [the regatta]'. However, there were some places where sliding booms allowed the pleasure boats to pass on and off the course between the races. *The Field* later reported that 'the booms were a splendid success, and were as much appreciated by the occupants of the pleasure craft as by the oarsmen competing'. The regatta set a record when it came to attendance as more than 12,000 people arrived by train for the last day's races.

Of the Thames RC's boats, Howell was the only one who reached a final at the century's last regatta at Henley. On his way to the final in the Diamonds, Howell easily defeated W. M. Bright of Argonaut RC, Toronto, and then in his next race, Edward G. Hemmerde of Univer-

The Prince and Princess of Wales visited the 1887 Henley Royal Regatta. It was into this boating party young Guy Nickalls sculled in his first final of the Diamonds. From *The Graphic* on 9 July 1887 by the artist Sydney P. Hall.

sity College, Oxford. In the final, the American met his old rival from Vesta RC, Harry Blackstaffe, who, on his way to the final, had met fairly modest opposition from Charles V. Fox of Pembroke College and later, Saint George Ashe of Thames RC.

In a review of the final, the *Rowing Almanack* of 1900 wrote: 'It was a splendid struggle to the half distance, where the men were level, but Blackstaffe showed signs of exhaustion – to this his very short boat possibly contributed – so Howell drew away and ultimately won somewhat easily'. What the short report in the *Almanack* failed to mention was that Blackstaffe's 'signs of exhaustion' meant that when Howell, who was behind, after a few long spurting strokes, was level with Blackstaffe, the Vesta man stopped sculling, totally pumped out. 'Although Blackstaffe started again he had no chance of catching Howell, who won easily with four lengths in 8 min. 38 sec.' *The Times* reported in an article the day after the race, on 8 July. At least Blackstaffe won the London Cup again on 11 July, which might have been a small comfort to some extent for this great oarsman.

SUITABLE FOR HENLEY.

A suitable toilette for ladies visiting Henley Royal Regatta according to *The Sketch* on 5 July 1899.

In his first heat of the 1899 Diamonds, Howell easily defeated W. M. Bright of Argonaut RC, Toronto, Canada.

In Howell's second heat of the 1899 Diamonds, he had no problems beating Edward G. Hemmerde of University College, Oxford.

In the 1899 final of the Diamonds, Howell again met his old rival from Vesta RC, Harry Blackstaffe. The 1900 *Rowing Almanack* wrote: 'It was a splendid struggle to the half distance then Howell drew away and won with four lengths'.

Twenty days after winning the Diamonds, Howell was in his single scull at Putney Bridge ready to defend his title of the Wingfield Sculls. He had agreed to scull not one opponent, but two, Harry Blackstaffe and Charles Fox. It was the latter who took the lead after a hard dash, leading with a length at the London RC, ahead of Howell, who was only slightly in front of Blackstaffe. At Craven Steps, Fox was still in the lead, now a length ahead of Blackstaffe with the American another three-quarter of a length down. However, Blackstaffe was the first to reach the Mile Post in 5 minutes 20 seconds, with Howell two lengths down. At this stage, Fox had disappeared from the race after not having been able to keep up with his mad dash at the start. Blackstaffe was three lengths in front of Howell at the Crab Tree and kept the same lead passing Hammersmith Bridge.

At Chiswick Eyot, Howell was gaining on Blackstaffe, but after that, when both of the scullers reached rough waters, Blackstaffe managed to maintain his lead, which by Chiswick Church was one length. At the Thornycroft's boat works, both scullers were level. Then Howell left Blackstaffe in his wake, going over to the Middlesex side. By Barnes Bridge, the Thames man had a four-length lead sculling very strongly. Contentedly, Howell won by four and a half lengths in 23 minutes 7 seconds, which was ten seconds slower than his record time the previous year.

That summer, the Vesta sculler went abroad, to Amsterdam, where he won the Holland Beker – The Sculling Championships of the Netherlands. Fox went on to win the Oxford Sculls later that autumn.

Again, the American newspapers blissfully wrote about Hunting Howell, the sporting son of a successful businessman. On 26 August 1899, the *Harper's Weekly* – 'A Journal of Civilization' as the subtitle read – had an article about Howell. The article started on a patriotic note:

The foremost oarsman of England, and perhaps of the world, is an American, and a true, loyal American, yet very little is heard of him in our own country, except in an occasional news dispatch when he wins some big event, such as the 'Diamond Sculls,' or the 'Wingfields'. For two years Benjamin Hunting Howell, of New York city, has been the acknowledged greatest oarsman on the Thames, and is to-day the champion of all Great Britain, having again won the 'Wingfields,' an open event, and the greatest of the year.

The article went on to describe Howell's race against Ten Eyck in the Diamonds in 1897 and stated that Howell had one ambition, to have another chance at his former antagonist, 'as he feels that he has improved greatly since the last race'. This would never happen.

The article was accompanied by a photograph of the American in his single scull, wearing a white rowing cap with his club's initials 'TRC'. Studying the photograph, one can clearly imagine what an incredible reach Howell must have had with his long arms. Added to this, his powerful legs must have given his sculls an enormous drive through the water.

With his victories in both the Diamonds and the Wingfields two years in a row, Howell was by now a household name among the English rowing gentry. Newspapers wrote about him, but his name also began to show up in books on rowing not only as an example of a successful oarsman, but also as a sculler with a somewhat different rigged shell. In 1898, Rowe and Pitman had written in *Rowing*: 'Mr.

A photo of Hunting Howell in the *Harper's Weekly* in August 1899.

Howell, who competed for the Diamonds Sculls at Henley Regatta in 1897, having very long reach, felt that he pinched his boat even more than did most scullers. He tried longer riggers (5 ft. span), and not improbably one may partly attribute his pace to the fact that he had a better-rigged boat than most of his opponents'.

In 1899, Guy Nickalls wrote on the same matter in his chapter 'Sculling' in the book *The "House" on Sport*. When in general an amateur sculler at that time used a pair of sculls of 9 ft. 9 in. overall, the inboard measurements was 2 ft. 8 1/2 in. 'The present amateur champion, B. H. Howell, [...] sculled in 1897 with a span of 5 ft. and with sculls 9 ft. 10 in. overall, and 2 ft. 8 1/2 in. inboard, and in 1898 with a length of 9 ft. 10 in. overall, and 2 ft. 10 in. inboard, and a span of 4 ft. 11 in.', Nickalls wrote, and he continued, 'His success with this rig will, I propheey [sic], lead to a revolution as to rig, and also as to the pace and comfort of the future sculler'. Although Nickalls called Howell's method of rigging his boat 'a phenomenal success', Nickalls also added that Howell was 'an untidy, rather clumsy sculler and lacking in watermanship' yet the American was 'undoubtedly possessed of exceptional strength and stamina', Nickalls wrote.

Even though the career of Guy Nickalls as a sculling star was, by

WILLS'S CIGARETTES

"WINGFIELD SCULLS."
"Vanity Fair," 2nd Series Nº 48

Guy Nickalls in the British tobacco company Wills's Cigarettes card, No. 48, 1902.

then, five years old – as the winner of the Diamonds in 1894 – he was still regarded as one of the English scullers with the most beautiful combination of leg and bodywork. Nickalls was also known to say and write whatever was on his mind. His straightforward attitude on rowing matters had got him into trouble on several occasions, and would continue to do so to the end of his days.

Much later, Theodore Cook, the former editor of *The Field*, also wrote about Howell's rigging in his book *Rowing at Henley* (1919): 'B. H. Howell in 1897 had such a long reach that the 5ft. spread he used was then the equivalent of 4ft. 9in. with any one else, and he could perhaps have done better with the 5ft. 2 in. spread use'.

Better or not, Hunting Howell was on top of his game both in 1898 and 1899, being the holder of both the Diamonds and the Wingfields. But how long would his success last?

CHAPTER 7
1900: 'A Poor Affair'

The result of the first Boat Race of the twentieth century was a clear victory for the Light Blues. Dudley-Ward was president again and was backed up by some good oarsmen, including Etherington-Smith. The crew was coached by James B. Close. The crew had four oarsmen from First Trinity and four from Third Trinity, including the cox. The ninth member of the crew came from Peterhouse. Cambridge won by an astonishing twenty lengths in 18 minutes 45 seconds, the same brilliant record time the winning Oxford crew had had in 1893.

'In 1900, Tideway rowing was at a low ebb and both Thames and London were experiencing particularly bad runs', Page writes in *Hear the Boat Sing*. For the upcoming Henley Royal Regatta, on 4-6 July, the *Baily's Magazine of Sport & Pastimes* wrote in the July issue: 'Happily, B. H. Howell (Amateur Champion of England) is going to defend his title for the last-named trophy, and the famous old Cantab is going as strong as ever'.

However, when it was time for the Diamonds, Howell was not really feeling well. In a review of the races of the Diamonds, Brickwood wrote in the *Almanack* of 1901: 'Howell was palpably amiss from malarial fever – an old complaint – and looked very bad'. Reading it today, it might surprise us that Howell was suffering from an illness that we in our days associate with a tropical climate, but malaria fever was still common in certain parts of England at this time, as it also was in the United States.

In the first heat of the Diamonds, Blackstaffe beat the Frenchman

Hunting Howell on the British tobacco company Ogden's cigarettes card, A Series, No. 94, 1901.

Louis Prével of Club Nautique of Nice, but not without difficulty. The man who had held Blackstaffe's boat at the start had squeezed so hard that he made a hole in the canvas. Blakstaffe sculled the race with his boat half-full of water. In the next heat, Charles Fox, now sculling for Guards Brigade RC, defeated Saint George Ashe of Thames RC.

In the third heat, Howell was behind F. A. Boyton of the London RC but passed him at Fawley. Then the Thames man easily paddled away, winning in 9 minutes 28 seconds. The Oxonian Edward Hemmerde, University College, easily overpowered Fritz Miller of the Royal Sport Nautique, Brussels, in another heat.

In the next day's first heat of the Diamonds, Howell met Fox, who was several lengths ahead at Remenham Rectory. Fox then had a five lengths lead at Fawley Court Boathouse. Howell spurted and came level with Fox at the White House, passed him and won by two lengths in 9 minutes 1 second.

Next heat was Blackstaffe versus Hemmerde. Despite having raced earlier in the day in a club four for the Wyfold Cup, the Vesta sculler went out hard and led in the beginning of the race. But the earlier race took its toll on Blackstaffe. By Remenham Rectory, the University College sculler was ahead, finally winning by three lengths and a half, in 8 minutes 42 seconds.

In the final heat, Howell raced Hemmerde. The latter sculler had prepared well for the Diamonds. Edwin Brickwood wrote in the *Al-*

A stereoview card showing an eight race at Henley at the end of the 1890s.

manack of 1901, 'Hemmerde had been training carefully for the Diamonds, and was rowing better than on any previous occasion'.

In *The Record of Henley Royal Regatta – From its institution in 1839 to 1902* (1903) Herbert Thomas Steward gave a report of the race:

This was a desperate race from start to finish. Mr. Howell led for the first half of the race, and was half a length ahead at Fawley Court Boathouse, but at the three-quarter mile mark Mr. Hemmerde was a trifle in front, led by a half length at the White House, was clear at the lower end of Phillis Court, and led by two lengths opposite the Grand Stand. Mr. Howell, however, making a desperate finish, only lost by three-quarter of a length. Time 8 min. 42 sec.

Mr. Howell fell out of his boat on stopping. He had a bad attack of malaria in the early part of the week, which caused the weakness from which he suffered.

Neither Howell nor Hemmerde entered for the London Cup on 16 July, which easily went to Blackstaffe for the fourth consecutive year. As expected, the Diamond Sculls winner Hemmerde sent an entry for the Wingfields, but withdrew it later.

On 18 July 1899, the competitors in the trial heat for the Wingfields were Fox, Ashe and Blackstaffe. Fox won and two days later he raced Hunting Howell, the holder, for the championship title of

Hunting Howell's collection of prizes and trophies.

the Thames and Great Britain. The 23-year-old Fox, who was two years Howell's junior, had improved from last year's Wingfields, being trained by George Towns. Howell, who was still ill, led at the start, but soon Fox spurted and was well ahead at the Mile Post. Passing Hammersmith Bridge, Fox had a seven-length lead. After that, a newspaper later reported, 'the race was a poor affair'. Fox won in the new record time, at 22 minutes 54 seconds, which was two seconds faster than Howell's winning time in 1898.

After this race Hunting Howell retired from rowing and never competed in a boat again.

Epilogue

What happened to Hunting Howell and his fellow oarsmen after the Wingfield Sculls in July 1900? The following month, on 25-26 August, the Thames RC sculler Saint George Ashe made history when he, as the first Englishman, represented his country in the first Olympic rowing regatta, held on the river Seine in Paris. (There was supposed to have been a rowing regatta at the Olympic Games in Athens four years earlier, but it was cancelled due to bad weather.) Saint George Ashe easily won his first heat in the single sculls. In the third heat, the Frenchman Louis Prével, who had rowed at Henley earlier in the summer, won his heat. Both scullers advanced to the semifinals. In his semifinal heat, Ashe came in third, which technically meant that he was kicked out of further advancement. However, he protested — no records tell us why — whereupon the French organisers allowed him to advance to the final. Prével won his semifinal heat and proceeded to the final, where he was interfered with and capsized before crossing the finish line. The Frenchmen Hermann Barrelet and André Gaudin took the gold and silver medals, respectively, while Ashe took the bronze — Great Britain's first rowing medal in the Olympic Games. (Though it might be more correct to say 'a third place', as bronze medals were not handed out at these early Olympic Games.)

The year 1901 began on a sad note for Trinity Hall BC, when Henry Trevor-Jones suddenly died on 24 January, 45 years old.

For the 1901 Grand Challenge Cup at Henley, an overseas competitor showed up. It was a crew from University of Pennsylvania, coached by the professional Ellis Ward of the famous Ward brothers. Just as the Cornellians six years earlier had been kept under strict surveillance by their coach, so too were the young oarsmen from Penn. Again the English newspapers wrote about the Americans' odd stroke and their lack of body swing. In the final of the Grand, Penn raced against Leander, which had rounded up Burnell, Dudley-Ward, Goldie and Etherington-Smith among others. The American university boys led at first, but at the end it was Leander that crossed the finish line first.

After the regatta, the Americans travelled to Dublin to race a crew from Dublin University at Killarney. The Penn oarsmen won that race with ease.

With these Americans at Henley, there had been no jumping the gun at the start, no unsportsmanlike behaviour, no dispute and no arguments, but still many of the influential rowing men in England were unhappy with the 'foreigners' after the 1901 Henley Royal Regatta.

It had actually begun five years earlier, Christopher Dodd writes in *Henley Royal Regatta*: '*The Field*, the country gentleman's newspaper, was by this time the most prominent rowing paper [...which, in 1896] ran a leading article advocating that Henley be closed to all foreign crews on the grounds that it was unsuited as an international occasion'.

In the summer of 1901, the anti-foreign campaign started again. Dr. Warre, headmaster of Eton, wrote in *The Times* that foreign entries were a threat to the amateurism at Henley. Rev. Charles J. Bristowe, who had rowed at Trinity Hall during some glorious years and was a Cambridge winning Blue in 1886 and 1887, wrote a letter to *The Field* where he voiced his opinion that it was good for the English oarsmen to race against foreign, also American, crews at Henley as there were lessons to be learned by doing so.

The 'Letters to the Editor' sections in *The Times* and *The Field* became battle grounds both for and against foreigners racing at Henley. On 7 August 1901, *The New York Times* quoted a letter from Sir Charles Dilke to *The Weekend*. Under the headline "Plea for American Oarsmen", Sir Charles, who in 1897 had come to Howell's aid, was quoted writing:

I have no right to interfere in this Henley controversy, but like every one who is concerned generally with our position in the world, I have the right to ask them that the 'foreigner' be not excluded from the Grand Challenge Cup without at least the simultaneous institution, by an equally high authority, preferably the Stewards themselves, of a competition, if not annual, at least triennial, under conditions which will induce the 'foreigner' to come. To exclude Americans would be difficult and ungracious. A distinguished American friend of mine two years ago was champion sculler – Hunting Howell (B. H. Howell of New York). He had no connection with this country till he came to Trinity Hall, (Cambridge University). He was one of the crew which narrowly beat Cornell for the Grand [sic]. Are we to 'row' Americans, and then forbid them to row against us? [...]

William (later 1st Baron Desborough) Grenfell, who had rowed for Oxford in the famous dead heat race in 1877 and in the winning crew of 1878, came up with a motion for the Henley Stewards which meant that overseas crews should be kept out of the regatta at Henley and that another suitable regatta should be created in England to host overseas competitors.

Grenfell immediately got positive response from Dr. Warre and Guts Woodgate, who then was president of Kingston RC, and also, a little surprising, from Harvard's former English coach, Rudie Lehmann.

However, another leading rowing authority at this time, Theodore Cook, was strongly against Grenfell's ideas and argued that only two foreign scullers and two crews had won cups at Henley up to that date: Columbia University (Visitors' 1878), Janus Ooms (Diamonds 1892), Nereus BC (Thames 1895) and Ned Ten Eyck (Diamonds 1897) – (again not including Irish crews' victories, nor including Hunting Howell's). Surely, Cook wrote, the English oarsmen were not afraid that the cups at Henley were all going abroad?

'Furthermore', Christopher Dodd writes, 'Cook outlined the difficulties of starting an international regatta [...] would foreigners come to it if they had other opportunities abroad and if they were told in no

Lord Desborough by 'SPY'.

uncertain terms that they were not wanted at Henley?' Dodd continues:

> The iconoclasts had ranged far and wide, suggesting abolition of the Thames Cup, a special cup for foreigners at Henley after which the winner would race the Grand winner over the championship course, criticizing the Americans for training too much and the English for training too little. Lehmann wanted to leave the colonials eligible, which Cook applauded, but he thought Lehmann's view of Henley to be a pleasant picnic rather than a regatta for first-class rowing.

Eventually, all major English rowing clubs were asked to make their voices heard on this matter. Later in November the same year, after the clubs had voted, it was clear that only Oxford University BC backed Grenfell's proposal, which there and then fell to pieces.

At the 1901 Diamond Challenge Sculls, Charles Fox defeated Saint George Ashe in the final. Fox did not defend his Wingfields title later that month, which instead went to Harry Blackstaffe, who also took the championship title in 1905, 1906 and 1908. He continued to be very successful in the Metropolitan Regatta's London Cup and added to his victories between 1897 and 1900 were his cup wins in 1901, 1903, 1904, 1905 and 1908.

Harry 'Blackie' Blackstaffe (on the right) was a well-liked oarsman. Not only was he a great sculler, but also a true 'club man', rowing in Vesta RC's pairs, fours and eights. Here is Blackstaffe in a pair with R. M. Hutchinson, who, after his rowing career was over, would become a famous figure on the music hall stage under the name Harry Tate. Blackstaffe has signed this post card and, as he many times did, added a drawing of a single sculler.

Blackstaffe also worked hard to take the Diamonds. He was the runner-up in 1905, but lost to Frederick S. Kelly, who won the race in the brilliant new record time of 8 minutes 10 seconds. Kelly had already won the Diamonds twice before, in 1902 and 1903. Nevertheless, it was Blackstaffe's turn in 1906 to take the Diamonds by defeating Captain William Darell of the Household Brigade BC.

Being victorious in the Diamonds, the Wingfields and the London Cup, Blackstaffe had one more big race to win. At the 1908 Olympic rowing regatta on the Henley course, each country was allowed to enter two crews in each event. As first boat in the single sculls, Great Britain selected the 20-year-old Alexander McCulloch of Leander, who had won the Diamonds that summer. The second entry was Blackstaffe, who, double the age of McCulloch, decided not to retire but to have a go at the Olympic single sculls title.

It was McCulloch and Blackstaffe who met in the Olympic single sculls final. It was a tremendous fight where both scullers lay side by side for most of the race. With 50 yards left to scull, the 40-year-old

Vesta sculler managed to get a canvas lead, which he held over the finish line.

In *Life's a Pudding*, Guy Nickalls humorously wrote that Blackstaffe was a sculler who 'improved with age', and that he 'never sculled better than he did at the Olympic Regatta of 1908'. It was also said that Blackie might not have been 'a pretty sculler', but he was, as Len Field wrote in his obituary about him in an autumn issue of the *Rowing* magazine in 1951, 'blessed with courage, determination and "guts" in the very highest degree'.

In the Olympic eights event Great Britain's first choice to represent the country was the winner of the 1908 Boat Race, Cambridge, which was stroked by Douglas 'Duggie' Stuart of Trinity Hall. He had stroked three victorious Light Blue boats in 1906, 1907 and 1908, even though he created a 'scandal' in his first race by rowing with a particularly ugly stroke, which came to be named after him, 'Stuart's sculling style'. Nevertheless, Cambridge only managed to take a third place in the Olympic eights.

Instead, it was the host nation's second boat that saved the honours in the eights. Harcourt Gold, who had rowed for Oxford in the Boat Race at four occasions, in 1896, 1897, 1898 and 1899 and now acted as coach, selected oarsmen from Leander to form the 'B crew'. Among them were some extremely good oarsmen, counting from the bow, Albert Gladstone, Frederick Kelly, Banner Johnstone, Guy Nickalls, Charles 'Don' Burnell (once known 'as the strongest sweep in England'), Ronald Sanderson, Raymond Etherington-Smith, Henry Bucknall and, as cox, Gilchrist Stanley Maclagan.

Due to some of the oarsmen's ages they were called the 'Old Crocks'. So at age 31, Etherington-Smith jokingly told his crew mate Nickalls, who was 42 years old: 'I suppose they have asked me because I am about half-way down the line between yourself and Bucknall in age' – Henry Bucknall, the stroke, was 23.

To not give the advantage of knowing the course beforehand, no foreign crews were allowed to compete at the 1908 Henley Royal Regatta, which was held less than a month before the Olympic rowing. (Apparently this rule did not apply to the British crews.) As the fine gentlemen they were, and the ones whom the British worried most about, the crew from Royal Club Nautique de Gand of Belgium, let it be known that they would not dream of entering Henley Royal Regatta that year to receive the benefit of knowing the course. They were busy back home in Ghent training for the Olympic regatta.

In 1906, a combination crew from two clubs in Ghent won the Grand Challenge Cup at Henley, and repeated the victory the following year (and again in 1909). Greg Denieffe has researched the Belgian crews these four years and writes about his findings in the entertaining article "The Mysterious Affair of 'Les Braves Belges'", published on the rowing history website 'Hear The Boat Sing' on 4 April 2014.

In the Olympic eights final, the 'Old Crocks' came to meet the Belgian crew. The following is an account of the race in *Henley Races* (1919) by Theodore Cook:

> This proved a magnificent race. The Belgians, who had twice won the Grand Challenge Cup at Henley, and at this Regatta had defeated Cambridge University, were thought likely winners by many people. [...] Along Temple Island both were rowing 38 a minute, Leander forging slowly ahead and having half a length to the good at the first signal-box. They gained another quarter length by the time the second box was reached, in spite of a fine spurt on the part of the Belgians. [...] At the Henley mile post Leander were rowing 35 a minute, and were a length and a quarter in front. Both crews rowed in to the finish very hard, Leander at 36 and the Belgians at 38 a minute, the former winning by a good two lengths' distance in the very fast time of 7 min. 52 sec.

On 3 September 2012, Raymond Etherington-Smith's 25g, 15 carat Olympic gold medal was auctioned off for an astonishing £17,500 ($27,738) at Christie's in London.

Hunting Howell's coach Bill East, who had been appointed a waterman to the Queen in 1898, became King Edward VII's Bargemaster, earning £60 a year, in 1901. Three years later, he published his how-to-book about oarsmanship, *Rowing and Sculling*.

Later in life, East became a landlord and was set up by his old pupil, the Hon. Rupert Guinness (Earl of Iveagh after his father's death in 1927), to run the Three Pigeons Hotel in Richmond, west of Lon-

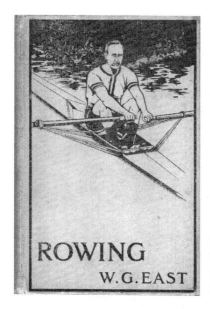

ROWING

W. G. EAST

In 1904, Bill East published his book *Rowing and Sculling*. While East got a nice spot on the cover of the book, the whole title would not fit.

don. Earl of Iveagh was president of the Thames RC between 1911 and 1967. It was a Thames sculler, the 23-year-old Jack Beresford, Jnr, who, in 1922, set a new record time for the Wingfields, polishing off Charles Fox's 1900 time (22 minutes 54 seconds) by 41 seconds.

As mentioned previously, George Towns became the world's professional sculling champion by beating Jacob Gaudaur in September 1901. In a race against Jim Stanbury in July 1905, Towns lost the title to his countryman, but regained it almost exactly a year later. Towns defended the title once more before he retired from the professional world championships by handing over the title to his brother, Charles, who lost it to William Webb of New Zealand in August 1907. Still the holder of the English professional title, George Towns travelled to London to face a challenge from Bill Barry's younger brother, Ernest, in October 1908. Ernest Barry, who was the Doggett's Coat and Badge winner in 1903, overpowered Towns, setting a new record time between Putney and Mortlake at 21 minutes 12,5 seconds.

Ernest Barry of Putney became the world professional champion in July 1912 by beating Richard Arnst of New Zealand. Barry was the first Englishman to hold the title since the Australian Ned Trickett had snatched it from Joe Sadler of Putney in June 1876.

Ernest Barry, the 1903 Doggett's Coat and Badge winner, took the English professional sculling championship title from George Towns in 1908. Four years later, Barry became the world sculling champion.

Rudie Lehmann, despite now being a married man, continued to coach Oxbridge crews until 1903. Having served as the Hon. Secretary of the Amateur Rowing Association (ARA) since 1893, he left this post in 1901, when he became the editor of the *Daily News*. This position seemed, however, to be stressful, so he stepped down from the editorship after a year. As a man with liberal views, Lehmann was strongly opposed to the Boer War, and after several failed attempts, in 1906 he was elected a Member of Parliament for the Liberal Party, a seat he held until 1910, when he did not seek re-election.

In 1902, Hunting Howell's name was mentioned in the New York newspaper *The Evening World*, which on 7 July wrote about the heats in the Diamonds at Henley. In the first heat C. S. Titus of the Union BC (New York) beat the Canadian Louis Scholes of the Don RC (Toronto) at 8 minutes 33 seconds, which the newspaper claimed to be one second faster than Howell's course record in 1898. Of course, this was wrong, as Howell's time had been 8 minutes 29 seconds. The winners in the other single sculls heats of the day were Julius Beresford, Kensington RC (father of Jack Beresford, Jnr), and Raymond Ethertington-Smith, Leander. The latter would be the runner-up, losing in the final to Frederick S. Kelly of Balliol College, Oxford (later of Leander Club).

It was also in or around 1902 that Hunting Howell married Augusta Clarion, a young lady who was nine years his junior and whom he had met in Paris. In 1905, their son Gerald Huntly Howell was born in the French capital.

According to a passenger list from the Ocean liner *Kronprinzessin Cecilie*, Hunting Howell arrived in New York from Southampton on 14 August 1907, but Augusta and Gerald are not mentioned on this voyage. Instead, their names come up six months later on a passenger list from the *Oceania*, which had left from Cherbourg, France, and arrived in New York on 6 February 1908.

The same year Howell founded the electric firm Garfield Manufacturing Company in Garfield, New Jersey.

According to the 1910 Census, the Howells lived in Pelham, a suburb of New York City, with servants: Gerald's governess Fanning, the Irish cook Kate Joslyn, French butler André Doremore and his French wife Louise, who was the maid.

In August 1911, Hunting Howell's mother, Katharine Van Liew Howell, passed away in London. It took some time to arrange her estate both in London and New York. On 3 December 1912, the *New York Tribune* published an article which said that the bulk of her estate went to Hunting Howell because 'he bestowed the kindest care upon her during her illness, while her son, Rapelje Howell, and her daughter, Miss Erla Louise Howell, the will stated, "quite neglected me"'. Hunting received $10,000 and real estate valued at $72,000. The article in the *New York Tribune* said that the house was at 140 West 57th Street in New York City, but in an article on 19 April 1913, in *The New York Times*, it stated that the address was 40 West 46th Street, both addresses quite smart.

To Hunting and Erla, their mother also left the leasehold on her

Frederick Septimus Kelly was born in 1881 in Sydney, Australia. He studied at Eton, where he rowed in the crew that took the 1899 Ladies' Challenge Plate at Henley. While at Balliol College, Oxford, Kelly began to scull and won the Diamond Sculls 1902, 1903 and 1905 (the two last victories for Leander Club). Kelly also took the Wingfields in 1903. As a member of Leander, Kelly also won the Grand in 1903, 1904 and 1905, and the Stewards Challenge Cup in 1906. He then resigned from rowing to concentrate on his music studies, but was called back to compete in Leander's famous crew, the 'Old Crocks', which became the 1908 Olympic champions in the eights. At the outbreak of the First World War, Kelly joined the Royal Naval Volunteer Reserve and was killed in the Battle of the Somme in November 1916. In April 2012, Kelly's 1905 Pineapple Trophy Goblet was sold at Bonhams in London for £3,800 ($6,225).

Opposite page: A striking beautiful Erla Louise Huntting Howell in a studio photograph taken in Cannes, France, in 1901. While Hunting was living a quiet family life in and around New York, his sister, Erla Howell, seemed to live a high-society life in London, Paris and the Riviera. Her name popped up now and then in *The New York Times*'s gossip column, which kept track of the American colonies in London and Paris. In 1916, the 40-year-old Erla married the fifteen year younger Italian Gaetano Nello de Facci Negratti in Milan, Italy. Two years later their daughter Liane Louise Negratti was born in Turin, Italy. During the 1920s, the Negrattis lived in London, and Erla's father, Frederick Howell, lived with them till he died in 1929. Four years later, Erla published a comedy in one act, *Babes in the World*, under the pseudonym "Nella Nagra". When Frederick Howell died, he left a magnificent collection of kaleido-

scopic paperweights to his son-in-law, who by then also had begun collecting paperweights, mostly of Italian and French origin. This fine collection of paperweights eventually went to Liane Louise, who in 1948 had married a French nobleman, Pierre Roissard, Baron de Bellet.

Erla Louise Howell Negratti passed away in 1975, 99 years old.

In May 2010, Bonhams in London auctioned off Baroness de Bellet's collection of paperweights. The nearly 200 pieces sold for an incredible £574,080 ($924,270).

house at 72 Brook Street in the heart of the fashionable Mayfair in London, just across the street from the famous Savile Club. In the will she also stated that her jewelry should go to Erla with the condition 'that she does not dispose of it in her lifetime to the daughter-in-law [...] Mrs. Florence Coates Howell, wife of Rapelje Howell'. Rapelje received the portrait that William Merritt Chase had painted of him as a child 'and all photographs of himself'. Katharine Van Liew Howell's husband, Frederick Howell, was not even mentioned in her will, according to *The New York Times*.

After the First World War, Hunting and Augusta Howell lived at Brooklands, Suffern, in New York State on the border of New Jersey. Not far away, they also had a summer house in Tuxedo Park, an area that attracted bankers, businessmen and others from the social elite. During the 1920s, the society columns in the New York newspapers were filled with gossip of what the residents at Tuxedo Park were up to, who was throwing a party and who were the guests, including 'Mr. and Mrs. Benjamin Hunting Howell'.

Then, there was the article "Forgotten Champion" in the issue of 2 July 1938 of *The New Yorker* when a reporter had knocked on the door of the ex-champion's flat at 145 East 52nd Street: 'He seemed surprised when we dropped in at his apartment, a comfortable furnished place with tapestried couches, embroidered fire screens, as he had resigned himself long ago to the fact that nobody knew there was a double winner of the Diamond Sculls on Fifty-second Street'.

Writing about Hunting Howell's victories in the Diamonds and the Wingfields, the article finished by saying:

Mr. Howell today is the head of the Garfield Manufacturing Company of Garfield, New Jersey, makers of electrical parts. He is still the same twelve stone eight. As of lack of recognition, he told us that at his age it doesn't make much difference. He lives a life of pleasant oblivion on Fifty-second Street and at Tuxedo Park, his summer home, where his racing trophies are stored. Only a few cronies know about his past. He hasn't been to a single rowing event since 1908, principally because none of his friends are crew fans. "It isn't fun to go alone," he says, with a faraway look in his eye.

On the same day that the article "Forgotten Champion" was published in *The New Yorker*, Joe Burk of the Penn Athletic Club, Philadelphia, won the Diamond Challenge Sculls in the new excellent record time, 8 minutes 2 seconds, taking eight seconds off Frederick S. Kelly's time from 1905. Burk was the fourth American to take the Diamonds, and he would repeat his victory the following year, 1939, being the last winner of the Diamonds before the Second World War put a six-year hold on the regatta. The next American to take the Diamonds during Howell's lifetime was Jack 'Kell' Kelly, Jnr, of University of Pennsylvania, who won in 1947 and 1949.

On 26 February 1953, Hunting Howell died at the age of 76. He was buried two days later at Sleepy Hollow Cemetery, New York.

Afterword

Early in my work on the 'Hunting Howell project', I received an e-mail from Frederick Elliott with information about where Howell is buried – Sleepy Hollow Cemetery in Sleepy Hollow, New York. Elliott's e-mail had the section and plot numbers of the oarsman's grave. For a long time I was planning to visit the cemetery, but it was only when I was done with my research and most of my writing, that I felt ready to visit Howell's grave. I contacted the administration of the cemetery to ask for directions within this large and famous cemetery. Jim Logan, superintendent of Sleepy Hollow Cemetery, came back right away saying that the section where Howell was laid to rest, section 29, is just inside the main gate on Route 9, then adding, that 'Howell is the only mausoleum in that section'.

Months later, on a beautiful sunny day, my family and I drove south on a busy I-95 to Sleepy Hollow, just over the border from Connecticut. Driving through the cemetery main gate we took a right and there, on a small hill, was the only mausoleum we could spot. Getting closer, Ellen, my wife, could read what it said over the doors of the mausoleum: 'Hunting-Howell'. While our daughter, Ingrid, age 12, refused to leave the car – she vividly remembered the story of the Headless Horseman which had really spooked her – our 8-year-old son, Anders, and I got out of the car and started climbing the lichen-covered stone steps up to the mausoleum. Anders counted the steps, one-two-three-four... up to 29.

The author in front of the Hunting-Howell mausoleum at Sleepy Hollow Cemetery.

Standing in front of the mausoleum, I was surprised to find that it was smaller than I thought it would be. I peeked through the windows of the copper doors, weathered to a green patina. The burial chamber had room for six bodies. Mr. Logan had mentioned in his e-mail that there were five members of the family buried in the mausoleum, Hunting, his wife Augusta, who died in 1955, his mother, father and sister-in-law, Bonnie Summit Howell, Rapelje Howell's second wife, who died in 1949. I guess, the sixth space was reserved for Hunting's brother, who passed away in 1960, but according to Mr. Logan, Rapelje is buried at Woodlawn Cemetery.

Strangely, the last name of Augusta and Hunting's parents in the chamber are written Hunting Howell with one 't' in Hunting, while the oarsman's name is given as Benjamin Huntting Howell, with two 't's in Huntting. The family name above the doors of the mausoleum reads 'Hunting-Howell'.

The back of the Hunting-Howell mausoleum.

Up on the hill of the mausoleum, towards the west, one can see the Hudson River in the distance.

What a perfect burial ground for a champion oarsman.

When I had walked down the 29 steps from the mausoleum, to where the car was parked, I turned around one last time to look up at the Hunting-Howell mausoleum. After a long research, it really felt like my Hunting Howell story had come to an end on that wonderful spring day. Gratefully, I performed a short nod towards the mausoleum on the hill, before I got into the car.

Acknowledgement

I am grateful to a number of people who helped me during the research and writing of this little book. I must begin with the late Hart Perry, who enchanted me with stories about Hunting Howell and inspired me to do research on this remarkable oarsman. My thanks go to Frederick Elliott, who donated the Hunting Howell photo album to the National Rowing Foundation, and generously shared information about Howell that he had received from his extended family, the Brandis, who were relatives of the oarsman's niece, Juliette Katherine Howell Brandi – my warm thanks also to the Brandi Family.

I had a special group of rowing historians who, one way or another, gave me information along the not always straight course down to the finish line. They are: Chris Dodd, Bill Lanouette, Peter Mallory, Bill Miller and Tom Weil. I was also incredibly lucky to receive the assistance from two friends and HTBS-colleagues, rowing historians Greg Denieffe and Tim Koch, who helped me with facts about the Boat Race and Henley Royal Regatta. They also kindly read and corrected the manuscript. My warm thanks to all you rowing historians.

Other rowing specialists, who supported me in their respective fields and whom I would like to thank, are O. W. Hall-Craggs, Honorary Secretary of the Wingfield Sculls Committee; Julian Ebsworth, archivist and librarian at the London RC; Tim Wilson, archivist and club historian at Thames RC; Vincent McGovern of Vesta RC; Eloise Chapman, collections manager at the River & Rowing Museum; and Daniel Grist, Secretary of Henley Royal Regatta.

I also owe thanks to Dr. John F. Pollad, Fellow librarian and Fellow archivist at Trinity Hall; Robert Athol, archivist at Trinity Hall; Dr. Philip Ewels, Trinity Hall Boat Club Captain 2009-10; and Jim Logan, superintendent at Sleepy Hollow Cemetery.

Living far away from the waterways where Howell plied his oar and sculls, I count myself fortunate to live close to the G. W. Blunt White Library at Mystic Seaport. This library has an incredible collection of rowing books, literature and magazines. It also has extremely helpful staff, who are led by library director Paul O'Pecko, who personifies the institution's wonderful service to its patrons. Besides O'Pecko, two members of the front desk staff have to be mentioned, Maribeth Bielinski and Carol Mowrey, who always cheerfully assisted me. Thanks also to two of the Museum's photographers, Dennis Murphy and Andy Price, who at one point came to my aid.

I am thankful to the National Rowing Foundation for allowing me to reproduce and publish all the photographs in Hunting Howell's photo album in this book. My warm thanks also go to my friend and HTBS-colleague Hélène Rémond, who kindly supplied a photograph of me from the 2011 Henley Royal Regatta; to my friend and work colleague Dayna Carignan, who assisted me and gave good advice on my design questions; and to my friend Linda Holmquist Mengelbier, who read the manuscript at a late stage.

Finally, I am in deep debt to my family. My wife Ellen and my mother-in-law Lucie Teegarden both read the manuscript in different stages and corrected the language and pointed out weaknesses in the narrative and overall greatly improved the text and truly helped me to cross the finish line. I would also like to mention our young, wonderful children, Ingrid and Anders, who maybe not always understood why their father was tied to the computer or in other ways was not available to play games with them or participate in their activities. However, throughout this time, they both were good sports about it. My warmest thanks, affection and love to you all.

List of Illustrations

Page III: Benjamin Hunting Howell. Benjamin Hunting Howell's photo album (BHHPA). Courtesy of the National Rowing Foundation (NRF).

Page VIII: Bill East, his younger brother and Hunting Howell. BHHPA. Courtesy of the NRF.

Page 2: Benjamin Hunting Howell. BHHPA. Courtesy of the NRF.

Page 5: An advertisement in *The Century Illustrated Monthly Magazine*, August 1886. Author's collection.

Page 6: The Arms of Trinity Hall, Wills's Cigarettes, tobacco card, 1922. Author's collection.

Page 7: The Front Entrance of Trinity Hall, postcard, ca. 1900. Author's collection. The Front Court of Trinity Hall, postcard, ca. 1900. Author's collection.

Page 8: A bump at the Lent Races. Illustration in the article "Rowing at Cambridge", *The English Illustrated Magazine*, [unknown date] 1890. Author's collection.

Page 9: "The Oxford & Cambridge Rowing Match at Henley on Thames" by painter William Havell. Courtesy of the River & Rowing Museum.

Page 11: Rudie Lehmann. Illustration in the article "Rowing at Cambridge", *The English Illustrated Magazine*, [unknown date] 1890. Author's collection.

Page 15: "Look Ahead, Sir! Reminiscence of Henley Regatta", *The Graphic*, 31 July 1880. Author's colletion.

Page 21: "Henley Royal Regatta, 1898" by Lucien Davis. Author's collection.

Page 23: Charles Courtney. Author's collection.

Page 25: Rudy [sic Rudie] Lehmann by 'SPY'. Author's collection.

Page 27: The Henley Course in *Rowing* (1898).

Page 28: The defeat of the Cornell University in the 1895 Grand Challenge Cup by Sydney P. Hall, *The Graphic*, 20 July 1895. Author's collection.

Page 30: The 1895 Cornell crew. Author's collection.

Page 33: Advice for a novice sculler. Author's collection.

Page 36: Sixteen oarsmen and two coxes wearing their 'Trial caps' for the Cambridge Trial eights race on 5 December 1896. BHHPA. Courtesy of the NRF.

Page 37: Dr. Edmond Warre by 'SPY'. Author's collection.

Page 42: Stanely Duff 'Muttle' Muttlebury. Illustration in the article "Rowing at Cambridge", *The English Illustrated Magazine*, [unknown date] 1890. Author's collection.

Page 45: Boat Race Course in *Rowing* (1898).

Page 46: The 1897 Light Blue crew. Author's collection.

Page 47: The 1897 Dark Blue crew. Author's collection.

Page 51: The 1898 Cambridge crew, *Punch*, 25 September 1897. Author's collection.

Page 52: 1897 Trinity Hall Double Sculls: Hunting Howell and Gerald Bullard. BHHPA. Courtesy of the NRF.

Page 53: The Trinity Hall crew, winners of the 1897 Head of the River. Published with kind permission of the Master and Fellows of Trinity Hall, Cambridge.

Page 54: Boathouse with American flag. BHHPA. Courtesy of the NRF.

Page 55: The 1897 Diamonds final race between Harry Blackstaffe and Ned Hanlan Ten Eyck by Henry Charles Seppings Wright, *The Illustrated London News*, 24 July 1897. Author's collection.

Page 58: William 'Bill' G. East. Allen & Ginter (N29), 1888. Author's collection.

Page 59: Hunting Howell and Bill East. BHHPA. Courtesy of the NRF.

Page 60: Vivian Nickalls. Author's collection.
The Hon. Rupert Guinness. Author's collection.

Page 61: Guy Nickalls. Illustration in the article "Rowing at Oxford", *The English Illustrated Magazine*, [unknown date] 1890. Author's collection.

Page 62: Walter Bradford 'Guts' Woodgate. From his autobiography *Reminiscences of an Old Sportsman* (1909).

Page 65: Hunting Howell resting in bed after his accident in October 1897. BHHPA. Courtesy of the NRF.

Page 66: Trinity Hall BC's Light Four, Michealmas term 1897. Published with kind permission of the Master and Fellows of Trinity Hall, Cambridge.

Page 69: William Dudley-Ward by 'SPY'. Author's collection.
William Fletcher by 'SPY'. Author's collection.

Page 70: Boat Race cox by Walter James, in R.P.P. Rowe and C.M. Pitman's *Rowing* (1898).

Page 71: Magdalene Pairs, Hunting Howell and Adam Bell in 1898. BHHPA. Courtesy of the NRF.

Page 72: May Week Tea Party in 1898. BHHPA. Courtesy of the NRF.

Page 74: Hunting Howell, a gentleman with an 'Oarsman's Degree', and fellow undergraduates. BHHPA. Courtesy of the NRF.
The 1898 Storks. BHHPA. Courtesy of the NRF.

Page 75: The 1898 Crescents. BHHPA. Courtesy of the NRF.
The 1898 Black & Whites. BHHPA. Courtesy of the NRF.

Page 76: Trinity Hall Ball Room in June 1898. BHHPA. Courtesy of the NRF.
The Trinity Hall Ball Stewards 1898. BHHPA. Courtesy of the NRF.

Page 77: After the 1898 Hall Ball. BHHPA. Courtesy of the NRF.
After the 1898 Masonic Ball. BHHPA. Courtesy of the NRF.

Page 78: Trinity Hall's eight losing to London RC in the 1898 Grand Challenge Cup. BHHPA. Courtesy of the NRF.
The first heat of the 1898 Diamonds, Hunting Howell beating A. F. G. Everitt. BHHPA. Courtesy of the NRF.

Page 79: The second heat of the 1898 Diamonds, Howell beating H. W. Stout. BHHPA. Courtesy of the NRF.
The final heat of the 1898 Diamonds, Howell beating Harry Blackstaffe. BHHPA. Courtesy of the NRF.

Page 80: Hunting Howell's 'pilot boat' for the 1898 Wingfields. BHHPA. Courtesy of the NRF.

Page 81: The start of the 1898 Wingfields. BHHPA. Courtesy of the NRF.

Page 82: 1898 Wingfields: a view from the steamer. Blackstaffe ahead. BHHPA. Courtesy of the NRF.
1898 Wingfields: getting close to Barnes Bridge. BHHPA. Courtesy of the NRF.

Page 83: 1898 Wingfields: about going under Barnes Bridge. BHHPA. Courtesy of the NRF.

Page 84: An article in *The Illustrated London News* (unknown date, July 1898) about the 1898 Wingfield Sculls. Author's collection.

Page 85: The 'American Champion of England', *The Deseret News*, 10 September 1898. Author's collection.

Page 86: The 1898 Silver Goblets: W. Fernie and 'Bogie' Bogle beating A. Hutchinson and S. Fairbairn. BHHPA. Courtesy of the NRF.

Page 88: George Towns, Ogden's cigarettes card, A Series, No. 99, 1901. Author's collection.

Page 89: Jacob Gaudaur, Allen & Ginter sports cards, series N28, No. 23, 1887. Author's collection.

Page 91: The Prince and Princess of Wales at the 1887 Henley Royal Regatta by Sydney P. Hall. *The Graphic,* 9 July 1887. Author's collection.

Page 92: A suitable toilette for ladies at the 1899 Henley Royal Regatta, *The Sketch*, 5 July 1899. Author's collection.

Page 93: The first heat of the 1899 Diamonds, Howell defeating W. M. Bright. BHHPA. Courtesy of the NRF.
The second heat of the 1899 Diamonds, Howell beating Edward G. Hemmerde. BHHPA. Courtesy of the NRF.

Page 94: The 1899 Diamonds final, Howell beating Harry Blackstaffe. BHHPA. Courtesy of the NRF.

Page 96: Hunting Howell. *Harper's Weekly*, 10 August 1899. Author's collection.

Page 97: Guy Nickalls. Wills's Cigarettes card, No. 48, 1902. Author's collection.

Page 99: Hunting Howell, Ogden's cigarettes card, A Series, No. 94, 1901. Author's collection.

Page 100: A stereoview card showing an eight race at Henley at the end of the 1890s. Author's collection.

Page 101: Hunting Howell's collection of prizes and trophies. BHHPA. Courtesy of the NRF.

Page 105: Lord Desborough by 'SPY'. Author's collection.

Page 106: Harry Tate and Harry Blackstaffe, postcard. Author's collection.

Page 109: The cover of Bill East's book *Rowing and Sculling* (1904).

Page 110: Ernest Barry, in 1912. Author's collection.

Page 112: Frederick Septimus Kelly. Author's collection.

Page 113: Erla Louise Huntting Howell, a studio photograph taken in Cannes, France, 1901. Author's collection.

Page 117: Hunting Howell's grave at Sleepy Hallow Cemetery. Author's collection. Photo: Ellen Buckhorn.

Page 118: The back of the Hunting-Howell mausoleum. Author's collection. Photo: Ellen Buckhorn.

Page 139: Photo: Hélène Rémond.

Bibliography

Ackroyd, Peter, *Thames: The Biography* (New York, 2007)

Anderson, Andy, *The Complete Dr. Rowing* (Groton, MA, 2001)

Applebee, L.G., *The Vesta Rowing Club 1870-1920* (London, [1920])

Atchinson, George T. & Brown, Geoffrey C., *The History of the Christ's College Boat Club* (Cambridge, 1922)

Ball, W.W.R., *A History of The First Trinity Boat Club* (Cambridge, 1908)

Birley, Derek, *Sport and the Making of Britain* (Manchester, 1993; paperback 1996, 2001)

Blandford-Baker, Mark, *Upon The Elysian Stream: 150 Years of Magdalen College Boat Club, Oxford* (Oxford, 2008)

Bolland, R.R., *Victorians on the Thames* (Tunbridge Wells, Kent, 1974)

Bond, Henry, *A History of the Trinity Hall Boat Club* (Cambridge, 1930)

Bourne, Gilbert C., *A Text-Book of Oarsmanship with an Essay on Muscular Action in Rowing* (London, 1925)

—, *Memories of an Eton Wet-Bob of the Seventies* (London, 1933)

Brickwood, E. D. (signature 'Argonaut'), ed., *Rowing Almanack and Oarsman's Companion 1898, 1899, 1900, 1901, 1930* (London)

Brittain, F. & Playford, H., *The Jesus College Cambridge Boat Club 1827-1962* (Cambridge, 1962)

Burnell, R.D., *Henley Royal Regatta: A Celebration of 150 Years* (London, 1989)

—, *Henley Regatta: A History* (London, 1957)

—, *The Oxford and Cambridge Boat Race 1829-1953* (London, 1954)

Burnell, R.D & Page, G., *The Brilliants: A History of the Leander Club* (Henley-on-Thames, 1997)

Claughton Scott, H., *The History of the Caius College Boat Club 1827-1927* (Cambridge, 1927)

Cleaver, Hylton, *A History of Rowing* (London, 1957)

Cook, Theodore A., *Henley Races* (London, 1919)

—, *Rowing at Henley* (London, 1919)

Deslandes, Paul R., *Oxbridge Men: British Masculinity and the Undergraduate Experience, 1850 – 1920* (Bloomington, IN, 2005)

Dodd, Christopher, *Henley Royal Regatta* (London, 1981)

—, *The Oxford & Cambridge Boat Race* (London, 1983)

—, *The Story of World Rowing* (London, 1992)

—, *Water Boiling Aft: London Rowing Club the First 150 Years 1856-2006* (London, 2006)

Dodd, Christopher & Marks, John (ed.), *Battle of the Blues: The Oxford & Cambridge Boat Race from 1829* (London, 2004)

Douglas, James, *Rowing on the Cam* ([Cambridge?], 1977)

Drinkwater, G. C., *The Boat Race* (London, 1939)

Durack, John & Gilbert, George & Marks, John, *The Bumps: An Account of the Cambridge University Bumping Races 1827-1999* (Cambridge, 2000)

East, W. G., *Rowing and Sculling* (London, 1904)

Encyclopædia of Sport, The, "Rowing", W.H. Grenfell, D.H. McLean, B. Fletcher Robinson, R.P.P. Rowe & Caspar Whitney (London, 1898)

Halladay, Eric, *Rowing in England: A Social History – The Amateur Debate* (Manchester, 1990)

Hempseed, B.W., *Seven Australian World Champion Scullers* (Christchurch, 2010)

Holt, Richard, *Sport and the British: A Modern History* (Oxford, 1989; paperback 1992)

Jones, Michael, *Michael Jones Guide to Henley Regatta & Reach* (Wokingham, 2001)

Kelley, Robert F., *American Rowing: Its background and Traditions* (New York, 1932)

Langstedt, Eric R., *The Rise of Cornell Rowing 1871-1920* (Newburgh, N.Y., 2012)

Lehmann, R. C., *Rowing in The Isthmian Library* (London, 1898)

—, *Selected Verse* (Edinburgh, 1929)

—, *The Complete Oarsman* (London, 1908)

Look, Margaret L., *Courtney: Master Oarsman – Champion Coach* (Interlaken, N.Y., 1989)

Magdalene Boat Club 1828-1928 (Cambridge, 1930)

Mumford, George S., "Rowing at Harvard" in *The H Book of Harvard Athletics 1852-1922*, edited by John A. Blanchard (Cambridge, MA, 1923)

Nickalls, G.O. & Mallam, P.C., *Rowing* (London, 1939)

Nickalls, Guy (G.O. Nickalls, ed.), *Life's A Pudding* (London, 1939)

—, "Sculling" in *The "House" of Sport: By Members of the London Stock Exchange, Vol. II*, compiled and edited by W.A. Morgan (London, 1899)

Nickalls, Vivian, *Oars, Wars and Horses* (London, 1932)

Page, Geoffrey, *Hear the Boat Sing: The History of Thames Rowing Club and Tideway Rowing* (London, 1991)

Pagnamenta, Peter (ed.), *The Hidden Hall – Portrait of a Cambridge College*, of special interest: Julian Ebsworth's "A Boat Club Saga" (London, 2004)

Peacock, Wadham, *The Story of the Inter-University Boat Race* (London, 1901)

Pisano, Ronald G. (Completed by Carolyn K. Lane & D. Frederick Baker), *William Merritt Chase: Portraits in Oil Volume 2* (New Haven, 2006)

Ripley, Stuart, *Sculling and Skulduggery: A History of Professional Sculling* (Sydney, 2009)

Ross, Gordon, *The Boat Race: The History of the First Hundred Races between Oxford and Cambridge* (London, 1954)

Rowe, R.P.P & Pitman, C.M., *Rowing [and Punting by P.W. Squire] in The Badminton Library* (London, 1898)

Seaman, Owen, *Horace at Cambridge* (London, 1895; 2nd ed. 1902)

Sherwood, W.E., *Oxford Rowing: A History of Boat-Racing at Oxford from the Earliest Times with a Record of the Races* (Oxford, 1900)

Steward, Herbert Thomas, *The Record of Henley Royal Regatta – From its institution in 1839 to 1902* (London, 1903)

Sparkes, D.I., *A History of the Trinity Hall Boat Club and Club Records 1949/50-1986/87* (Cambridge, 1988)

Underwood, Lynn (ed.), *Henley Royal Regatta 1839-1989* (Tewesbury, [1989?])

Weightman, Gavin, *London's Thames – The River that Shaped a City and its History* (New York, 2005)

Weil, Thomas E., *Beauty and the Boats – Art and Artistry in Early British Rowing* (Henley-on-Thames, 2005)

Wells, H.B., *Vesta Rowing Club: A Centenary History* (London, 1969)

Wigglesworth, Neil, *The Social History of English Rowing* (London, 1992)

Woodgate, Walter B., *Reminiscences of an Old Sportsman* (London, 1909)

Young, C.V.P. *Courtney and Cornell Rowing* (Ithaca N.Y., 1923)

—, *The Cornell Navy 1871-1906: A Review* (Ithaca, N.Y., 1907)

129

Magazines & Newspapers

Baily's Magazine of Sport & Pastimes: Vol. 74, July 1900

Black and White: 20 March 1897

Black and White Budget: 28 September 1901: A. Wallis Myers, "The King's Watermen"

Brooklyn Eagle: 23 February 1902: "Obituary: Mrs. B.H. Howell"

Cambridge Review, The: 26 November 1896; 29 April 1897

Carloviana 2012 [journal published by the Carlow Historical and Archaeological Society], May 2012: Greg Denieffe, "The Rowing Bunburys: Their Races and Their Rowing Contemporaries"

Chester Times: 4 September 1928

Collier's: October 2012: A. Anthony Howell, "The Sugar Men"

Cornell Daily Sun, The: 2 July 1897: "Mr. Lehmann Speaks at the Harvard Commencement Dinner"

Cornell Magazine, The: December 1894 (Vol. VII, No. 3): Horation S. White, "The Henley Regatta"

Country Life Illustrated: 18 February 1897; 8 May 1897; 5 June 1897

Deseret News: 10 September 1898

Electrical Review, The: 8 September 1899; 13 December 1899

English Illustrated Magazine, The: [unknown month] 1890

Evening World, The: 7 July 1902: "Union Boat Club Champion Beats Scholes, of Toronto, in Preliminary for Diamond Sculls at Henley"

Graphic, The: 9 July 1887; 20 July 1895; 30 July 1898

Harper's Weekly: 20 July 1895; 26 June 1897; 26 August 1899

Harvard Crimson, The: 7 April 1898: "Mr. Lehmann Arrives"; 10 December 1901: E.C. Storrow & F.L. Higginson, "The Record in Rowing"

Illustrated London News, The: 24 July 1897; [unknown date] July 1898

Log of Mystic Seaport, The: Vol. 56, No. 1, 2005: Göran R Buckhorn, "Charles Courtney and the Decline of Professional Sculling in America"

Los Angeles Herald: 10 September 1899: "An American Every Inch"

Mercury, The: 22 May 1911

New Yorker, The: 2 July 1938: "Forgotten Champion"

New York Evening Post: 6 July 1925

New York Times, The: 10 July 1895: "Cornell Gets a Heat"; 12 July 1895: "Where Fairly Beaten: Cornell's Statement about the Race with Trinity Hall – Regretted Leander did not Start"; 29 March 1896: "A Great Varsity Race"; 19 March 1897: "R.C. Lehmann Here Again"; 19 December 1897: "Oarsmen here from Europe"; 13 February 1898: "Split in the Cambridge Crew: B.H. Howell Denies Charges Brought Against Him by Dudley Ward"; 18 May 1898: "Cambridge Double Sculls"; 8 July 1898: "American Wins at Henley: B.H. Howell Captures the Diamond Sculls. Breaking Two records in a Day"; 14 September 1898: "Harvard's Coach Marries"; 6 July 1899: "The Regatta at Henley: B.H. Howell, the American, Wins a Heat for the Diamond Sculls"; 28 July 1899: "Another Victory for Howell"; 7 August 1901: "Plea for American Oarsmen"; 19 April 1913: "Must Keep Heirlooms"

New York Tribune: 3 December 1912: "Didn't Mention Husband: Bulk of English [sic] Woman's Estate Goes to 'Kind' Son"

Oarsman, The: January/February 1979: Thomas C. Mendenhall, "Coaches and Coaching (V): The British are Coming" [on Rudie Lehmann]

Oswego Daily Palladium, The: 20 July 1899: "People of the Day: Winner of the Diamond Sculls"

Outing: August 1897; [unknown date] September 1898; 1 April 1899

Oxford Magazine, The: 17 February 1897

Punch, or the London Charivari: 10 July 1886; 25 September 1897

Rochester Democrat and Chronicle: 17 April 1900

Rowing: Vol. 2, No. 28, First Autumn issue 1951: Len Field, "'Blackie' – A Tribute"

Rowing & Regatta: #39, December 2009: Göran R Buckhorn, "In this month" [on Frederick S. Kelly]; #49, January/February 2011: Göran R Buckhorn, "In this month" [on Hunting Howell]; #53, June/July 2011: Mike Rowbottom, "A Case Study in Perseverance" [on Harry Blackstaffe]

Sacramento Daily Union: 18 November 1899: "Big American Oarsman"

Sandow's Magazine of Physical Culture: July and August 1899: [signature R.P.L.] "Athletics of the Month"

Saturday Review, The: 27 March 1897: Charles W. Dilke ,"Two Fine Crews"

Sketch, The: 22 March 1893: Max Pemberton, "A Famous 'Varsity Coach: A Chat with R.C. Lehmann"; 5 July 1899

Star, The: 24 July 1899: "Anglo-Colonial Notes: George Town's [sic] Bad Luck"

Strand Magazine, The: No. 78, July 1897: S.J. Housley, "How a Racing Boat is Built"

Sydney Morning Herald, The: 5 September 1900: "Rowing"; 31 August 1901: "Rowing: The Sculling Championship"

Tatler, The: 5 March 1902: W.B. Woodgate, "The Making of a Rowing Blue"

Times, The: 12 July 1895: "Rowing: Henley Royal Regatta"; 18 November 1896: Rowing: Cambridge University (Colquhoun) Sculls; 1 February 1897: "Rowing: The University Boat Race"; 5 April 1897: "The University Boat Race"; 22 July 1897: "Rowing: The Wingfield Sculls"; 14 October 1897: "Accident to a Cambridge Oarsman"; 12 February 1898: "Rowing: Cambridge University Boat Club"; 14 February 1898: "Rowing: The University Boat Race"; 15 February 1898: "Rowing: The University Boat Race, Cambridge"; 8 July 1898: "Rowing: Henley Royal Regatta"; 26 July 1898: "Rowing: The Wingfield Sculls"; 6 July 1899: "The Regatta at Henley: B.H. Howell, the American, Wins a Heat for the Diamond Sculls"; 8 July 1899: "Henley Royal Regatta"; 28 July 1899: "Rowing: The Wingfield Sculls"; 19 July 1900; 21 July 1900; 16 November 1946: "The Rt. Hon. W. Dudley Ward" (obituary)

Vanity Fair: 18 July 1895: [by Walter B. Woodgate]; 16 July 1896: [by Walter B. Woodgate]

USRowing Magazine: November 1999: J. Arthur Rath, "Ten Eyck, The Undefeated Oarsman"

Websites

The Boat Race (www.theboatrace.org)

Friends of Rowing History (www.rowinghistory.net)

'Hear The Boat Sing' (www.heartheboatsing.com)

Henley Royal Regatta (www.hrr.co.uk)

River & Rowing Museum (www.rrm.co.uk)

Trinity Hall, Cambridge (www.trinityhall.cam.ac.uk)

Where Thames Smooth Water Glide (www.thames.me.uk)

Wikipedia (www.wikipedia.org)
"His Majesty (comic opera)"

"The Rower of Vanity Fair":
Crum, Walter Erskine
Dilke, Charles Wentworth
Dudley-Ward, William
Etherington-Smith, Raymond Broadley
Fletcher, William Alfred Littledale
Gold, Harcourt Gilbey
Grenfell, William Henry (Lord Desborough)
Guinness, Rupert Edward Cecil Lee (Lord Iveagh)
Hemmerde, Edward G.
Lehmann, Rudolf Chamber
McLean, Douglas Hamilton
Muttlebury, Stanley Duff
Nickalls, Guy
Stuart, Douglas Cecil Rees
Warre, Edmond

Index of People

Page numbers in italics refer to the illustrations.

137

Wack, Henry Wellington, 20
Ward, Ellis, 103
Ward, Leslie (signature 'SPY'), *25, 37, 69, 105*
Warre, Edmond, 37, *37,* 103, 104
Warre, Felix, 70
Washington, George, 2
Wauchope, David A., 24
Webb, William, 109
Wethered, Frank, 83
Whigworth, A., 40
White, Horation S., 18, 19
Wigglesworth, Neil, 57
Willan, Frank, 24, 26, 29, 45
Wingfield, Henry C., 31, 81
Winship, W., 57
Wood, Matt, 39
Woodgate, Walter 'Guts', 49, 61, 62, *62,* 104
Woodroffe, William H.G., 34, *36*
Wray, James, 90
Wright, Henry, 66
Wright, Henry Charles Seppings, *55*

A Note about the Author

Göran R Buckhorn, a Swede living in Connecticut, is a magazine editor, freelance culture scribe and rowing historian. Buckhorn began to row in the 1970s at the local rowing club in his hometown of Malmö in the south of Sweden.

Already in March 1979, he saw his first published article in a newspaper, a piece about The Boat Race. In 1990, Buckhorn and his rowing mate Per Ekström founded the Swedish rowing magazine *Svensk Rodd* and co-edited it for ten years. After moving to America in 2000, Buckhorn was a contributing editor to the magazine until it ceased to exist in late 2014.

Throughout the years, Buckhorn has written numerous articles on rowing for books and magazines, for example the British *Rowing & Regatta*, in which he for a short stint had a rowing history column. In 2000, he published a book with six essays and articles on rowing in Swedish, *En gång roddare... [Once a Rower...]*

Buckhorn is one of the Directors of Friends of Rowing History and a member of BARJ, the British Association of Rowing Journalists.

In March 2009, he founded the rowing history blog 'Hear The Boat Sing' (HTBS), which these days publishes contributions from the foremost rowing historians and writers in the world.

Made in the USA
Lexington, KY
07 December 2015